The Awakening

By
The Viking Buddha

Copyright © 2024 by The Viking Buddha

ISBN: 978-1-917129-96-1

All rights reserved. No part of this book may be reproduced or used in any manner without written permission of the copyright owner except for the use of quotations in a book review. For more information, your details for contact here.

Contents
Contents
Acknowledgements
Disclaimer
About the Author
Introduction 1
PART 1: FROM PAIN TO POWER
Chapter 1: Stress 3
Chapter 2: Mental Health 13
Chapter 3: Alcohol & Substance Abuse 27
Chapter 4: Narcissistic Abuse 38
Chapter 5: Bullying 46
Chapter 6: Trauma 53
Chapter 7: Forgiveness 58
Chapter 8: Gratitude 61
Chapter 9: Family & What's Important 65
Chapter 10: Cancer 70
Chapter 11: Alkaline Nutrition 93
Chapter 12: Talk Therapies 96
Chapter 13: Power of Hypnosis 100
Chapter 14: Cold Water Therapy 104
Chapter 15: Complementary Therapies 106
PART 2: THE KEY TO YOUR LIFE
Chapter 16: Mindfulness/Shinrin Yoku 124
Chapter 17: Ho'oponopono 135
Chapter 18: Neuroplasticity 140
Chapter 19: Quantum Embodiment 146
Chapter 20: Epigenetics 151
Chapter 21: The Enneagram 158
Chapter 22: The Key to Your Life 169
Chapter 23: Life Purpose Quest 175
Chapter 24: Your Ikigai 182
PART 3:' THE AWAKENING'
Chapter 25: Universal Law 190
Chapter 26: Law of Attraction 195
Chapter 27: Reality Transmuting 203
Chapter 28: The Millionaire Mindset 213

Acknowledgements

I would like to say a few thanks to a few people who have made this book possible.

Thank you to my children, Shane, Shannon, and especially to the three younger ones, Cheyenne, Cheroken, and Cielo, as they have been so patient while I have been setting up The Viking Buddha business and writing this book.

To my mum who never ceases to amaze me, and for all her support, to my dad who passed away in 2010, for all his support over the years which made me who I am today. Also thanks to Michael, and Helen, for all their support whilst writing this book,

Also many thanks to all the nurses, health care assistants and support workers I have worked with over the years on ward 12, and the amazing team we had on there, CIU, and ECS, at Blackpool Hospital, and also at The Harbour Blackpool.

DISCLAIMER

Although the author and publisher have made every effort to ensure that the information in this book was correct at press time, the author and publisher do not assume and hereby disclaim any liability to any party for any loss, damage, or disruption caused by errors or omissions, whether such errors or omissions result from negligence, accident, or any other cause.

This book is not intended as a substitute for the medical advice of physicians. The reader should regularly consult a physician in matters relating to their health, particularly with respect to any symptoms that may require diagnosis or medical attention.

ABOUT THE AUTHOR

The Viking Buddha, aka David Bentley, started his interest in the mind and therapy while studying psychology. In 2004 he trained as a Clinical Hypnotherapist and Stress Management Consultant. In 2005 he trained to be an Holistic Therapist, Massage Therapist and Clinical Reflexologist. He worked as a therapist in Burnley and also in Co. Cork Ireland, before returning to Blackpool UK in 2009 after his marriage ended. In 2011, he started working at Blackpool Hospital and worked there for nine years before leaving in 2020. He has also worked at a Mental Health Hospital in Blackpool.

He has further wanted to expand his knowledge by training in talk therapies such as Trauma Therapy, CBT. DBT/SFBT/REBT/NLP, Psychotherapy, Gestalt Therapy, and a number of other talk therapies, in addition to a number of Life Coaching qualifications.

He has a special interest in Mental Health, Trauma, and Alcohol and Substance Abuse, and he has taken further qualifications in Mental Health over the years.

He started The Viking Buddha business in 2023 to try and help as many people as he could, and in addition to this book, he has workshops, groups, and retreats planned from summer 2024 onwards.

Introduction

Namaste, Aloha, and Hello and welcome to 'The Awakening', from The Viking Buddha.

Now I am guessing some of you are thinking, why The Viking Buddha? It was actually thought of whilst walking in the middle of nowhere with a friend and I was thinking what could I call myself and the therapy business? Now, of course, I have the beard, and my ancestry is 41% English, and 59% North Western European, and I have Scandinavian Ancestors, and have kind of been into the Norse way of life all my life. The Buddha part comes from my deep spirituality, and at the time of writing if you rubbed my belly you might have some good luck come your way.

With regards to the book itself, it actually goes side by side with the three day 'The Awakening 'Workshop which we run. Part one, is From Pain to Power, as we discuss things that may be holding you back such as Mental Health, Stress, Illness, Trauma, Substance abuse, and what is really important in life.

Part two is 'The Key to Your Life', and this part starts by discussing what we are, and how powerful and intelligent our minds and body's really are, with an iintroductory dive into Epigenetics, Neuroplasticity, and the fascinating world of Quantum Physics. Then we look into discovering your life with your Life Purpose and Ikigai. Part three, is about the Law of Attraction, Universal Law, and how to manifest the life you really want.

This book is about Eastern Medicine, Alternative Medicine, spirituality, and what we really are, which is energy. It is on the absolute opposite spectrum to Western Medicine and Pharmaceutical Companies, and is about healing yourself naturally, and breaking from old conditioning and the Matrix, and discovering YOUR true potential.

The book itself is a basic introduction into all of these subjects in the chapters -, if I were to go into each subject in depth, there would be a number of volumes of the book. The Viking Buddha does offer more in-depth workshops in many of the subjects in the book where we go much deeper, and of course, the three-Day Workshop and dates for these will be available soon on the website which is www.thevikingbuddha.com

Part One
From Pain
To Power

Chapter 1
Stress

We all go through stress at different times in our lives. Stress can be good for us in certain situations, but when out of control and negative, it can cause serious problems in our lives and is very much a big factor in our bodies breaking down and the start of dis-ease in our bodies.

So, what is Stress?

As I said above, Stress isn't all bad, in fact, we couldn't survive without it, as it helps us to adapt to our environment, and when we face challenges, it can help us meet these challenges and overcome them.

When the body experiences acute stress, there are a range of physiological responses that occur to prepare us for what we call the 'fight or flight 'response. Our respiration increases, our heart rate increases, nutrients are mobilised the immune system is activated, and our awareness heightens. At the same time as all of this is happening, our body also starts to divert resources which are being used for different processes in our body such as digestion and reproduction etc, and these are diverted to this fight or flight response and immediate survival. This perfectly regulated response to stress provided our ancestors with the energy they needed to survive in dangerous environments.

When stress is beneficial to us, it is named 'eustress 'or positive stress, and this kind of stress can motivate us., it can give us more focus, and more energy, can improve functions, and enhances our ability to thrive in the environment we are in.

But what happens when stress exceeds your capacity and ability to cope? It becomes 'distress', negative stress. This makes the person feel unpleasant, often decreases performance, and can lead to mental, emotional, and physical problems. Prolonged distress can lead to the breakdown of the body and dis-ease, and there are links to long-term stress with cancer. We will go into this in much more detail in a chapter further down the line in the book.

Stress in many ways is like turning on a superpower, it is getting your body ready to take on a challenge such as surviving, exceeding, or conquering whatever problem comes your way.

Stress is an automatic reaction which can help you perform at your best. When stress is being used in a good way it is like pressing a button for ultimate power.

So what happens during the stress response?

When the body perceives a stressor, the Hypothalamus-Pituitary-Adrenal (HPA) axis is activated. The axis consists of the Hypothalamus and Pituitary Gland which are located in the brain, and the adrenal glands, which are located on the top of the kidneys.

When this axis is activated, it causes the release of several different hormones such as cortisol and epinephrine (aka adrenaline). These orchestrate and govern the stress response.

The first stage of the stress response is called the alarm reaction. Cortisol is the hormone responsible for many of these physiological changes. The problem with this is that when cortisol production is too high for too long, numerous problems follow, such as health problems, anxiety, and depression.

The human body is constantly working to keep balance or homeostasis. Your body can recover very quickly from positive stress, but with distress (negative stress) your body cannot maintain homeostasis because the intensity and the frequency of the stressor exceed its capacity to cope.

Long-term distress can come in all sorts of ways including divorce, death of loved ones, financial problems, chronic injury or illness, and over long periods of time this is destructive. This is one of the main things that you need to get under control in your life, and in the later chapter about cancer, we will show why it is one of the main contributory factors in the formation of cancer in your body.

So, how does intense emotion cause the brain to form intense memories? It is well known that emotions can trigger a rise in stress hormones, and these hormones trigger activity in the amygdala. The amygdala increases memory-forming activity which engages the frontal lobes and what is called the basal ganglia to 'tag' these memories as important.

The problem with this can be that the memories are stored with more emotional and sensory details which can trigger rapid unintended recall of these memories.

So what does the amygdala do?

Well it has a great deal to do with the fight or flight response as we have discovered, and it controls the release of adrenaline which is good for running away from tigers, but I am not sure you will be encountering many of them. What it does do, is it suppresses logical processing in the frontal lobe, it creates the 'fear 'sensation, it hijacks your logical thinking in favour of emotional response, and therefore it isn't so good for making decisions or communication.

So how do you know when you are stressed?

You will hear many people around you say they are stressed. But what does being stressed actually mean? What you really do need to know is how to control Stress.

Stress is like having a superpower, but if you can't control it, then you will crash, burn, and explode. But if you learn to control stress, you also learn how to use your power.

How do you know when you are stressed? Some of the symptoms of stress could be:-

- Your stomach goes round and you feel sick

- You want to cry
- You feel exhausted
- You can't sleep and are wide awake half the night
- You can't think straight
- Sweaty hands
- A feeling something bad is going to happen

What you need to start doing to control your stress is to Recognise and Realise when you are stressed.

Other signs of Stress can be rambling and ranting, bloodshot eyes, frazzled looks, and unkempt hair.

The next time you feel stressed about something, a good technique is to write down what you feel. Just write down and notice what comes from being stressed. You can only control your stress, when you start to recognise when you are getting stressed.

Stages of Stress

1. Recognise your challenger, this could be a text with bad news, or someone wanting to punch or hurt you. There are many challenges in life, and it is so important to recognise who and what your challenger is.

2. Stage two is about assessing the challenger. This is a lightning-fast reaction in your body, where you have to make a decision about how serious the challenge is to you. If it is someone a lot bigger than you about to punch you, then this is a very serious challenge, but if it's something really small, then it is no challenge.

3. The next thing that happens is that your body mobilises your forces. When your brain assesses that this is indeed a serious challenge for you, it does all it can to prepare you to take the challenge on. This is when your brain activates your stress circuit, this is what is called the Hypothalmic-Pituitary-Adrenal (HPA) Axis. It floods your body with energy, sugar, and glucose which provides immediate fuel to your muscles, to deal with the stress at hand. There are a number of other things that happen with your body during this time when your body is preparing you to deal with a very stressful incident:

Your heart beats faster and you start to breathe faster. Your blood is taken away from your digestive system and rushes into muscles and brain. Your body releases painkillers, and this is all done to protect you from injury. It also dilates the pupils in your eyes so you can see better, and also sharpens your senses so you can act faster and be stronger.

4. This is where we face the challenger, as we have the heightened perception, stamina, and energy to deal with the problem.

5. This is where we go into recovery, and where the brain starts to calm the body down. Your heartbeat starts to slow down, your breathing goes back to normal and releases hormones such as oxytocin which make you more sociable so you might be able to talk about what happened.

Stress can be a positive, and can be a lifesaver if you are about to do something difficult such as performing, exams, sports etc.

The problem is we get stressed due to everyday life, work, when minor things come up, when we don't have a challenger, and this is where stress becomes a problem.

When we get stressed like this, our body does all of the above, and we are filled with this energy and there is no outlet.

Many times we get stressed over the smallest things, and things which are way down the line such as an exam, or work that needs to be done, so you can't use the energy from the stress response to deal with anything, you just sit burning, and eventually blow up.

We need to learn how to turn on and also turn OFF the stress button.

Stress is designed to help you perform and act now. For example, if you have an exam in a few weeks, could you use your stress to help you revise now? You need to redefine it to something you can take on NOW, and not worry about what is down the line.

A fantastic way to deal with stress is something called the STOP technique. It is a tool which can be used when something has just happened that you feel you need to react to, and you are feeling very strong emotions. The idea of this technique is to give yourself a few seconds or minutes to STOP and PAUSE and take that time to decide how you want to respond, rather than react.

1. STOP: make the decision to not react, but instead, pause
2. TAKE YOUR TIME: breathe… just breathe and bring all of your attention to just breathing for a moment. Count each breathe until you reach five, and take this time to focus on your breathing and then
3. OBSERVE: observe what is going on for you right now, what are you feeling in your body? No judgement, just observe.
4. PROCEED: decide how you want to proceed in the next minute. Don't make any decisions about the big picture, or what you want to do in the coming days and weeks, but what you want to do in the next few minutes now that you have had time to take a step back. Maybe doing nothing, not taking any action or even walking away, or consciously responding to the problem. Make a conscious decision about how you want to respond, rather than automatically reacting to the situation.

How does stress affect the body?

Stress can affect the body in so many different ways, so it is very important you start to learn how to control your stress and don't let things get to you. Later in the book we discuss mindfulness, and being in the present moment, and this is so important.

Some of the effects stress can have on your body are:
- Skin:- acne, psoriasis, eczema, dermatitis, and skin rashes.
- Stomach:- peptic ulcers, inflammatory bowel disease, stomach cramps, acid reflux, nausea, and weight fluctuations.
- Pancreas:- elevated secretions of insulin, diabetes, damaged arteries, and obesity.
- Immune system:- immune suppression, increased inflammation, chronic health conditions including cancer.
- Head:- mood swings, depression, anger, irritability, lack of energy, concentration problems, anxiety, panic attacks.
- Heart:- increased blood pressure, increased heart rate, higher cholesterol, and increased risk of heart attack and stroke.

- Intestines:- decreased nutrient absorption, reduced metabolism, inflammatory bowel disease.
- Reproductive system:- reduced fertility, erectile dysfunction, low libido
- Joints:- aches and pains, inflammation, tension, lowered bone density, tightness in muscles and joints.

Your body can recover quickly from positive stress, but with negative stress (distress), your body cannot maintain homeostasis if the intensity or frequency of the stressor exceeds its capacity to cope.

If the neurotransmitters such as dopamine, norepinephrine, and serotonin have been depleted, the brain will search for ways to get back to balance through actions or inactions that flood the body with feel-good chemicals to meet those needs.

- Low Dopamine:- no motivation, no interest, impatient, inattentive, boredom, addictions, impulsive, and forgetful.
- Low Serotonin:- overwhelmed, worried, anxious, regretful, sorrowful, resentful, needy, moody, over-giving, and rigid.

Grumpy old lady

A young lady sat on a bus, at the next stop a loud and grumpy old lady came and sat by her ... she squeezed into the seat and bumped her with her numerous bags.

The person sitting on the other side of the young lady got upset and asked her why she didn't speak up or say anything.

The young lady responded with a smile," It is not necessary to be rude or argue over something so insignificant, the journey is so short, I get off at the next stop."

This response deserves to be written in GOLDEN letters.- "It is not necessary to argue over something so insignificant, our journey together is so short."

If each of us realised that our time is so short, and to darken it with quarrels, futile arguments, not forgiving others, discontentment, and a fault-finding attitude would be a waste of time and energy.

Did someone break your heart? Be calm, the journey is short. Did someone betray, bully cheat or humiliate you? Be calm, and forgive, the journey is so short.

Whatever troubles anyone brings us, let us remember that our journey together is short, no one knows the duration of this journey, and no one knows when their stop will come. Our journey is so short, let us cherish friends and family, let us be respectful, kind and forgiving to each other, and let us be filled with gratitude and gladness.

Life really is short. If people can start to live their own lives, and don't let others impact on their life so much, and get the most out of their own lives. You really don't know what is going on in someone else's life for them to act the way they do, so focus on yourselves, and being the best you can be, whilst trying to be kind to others.

Garbage Trucks

A man waved down a taxi and got in it to go to work. Along the way, a car pulled out and there was nearly an accident.

The man in the other car got out and was angry, and shaking his fists, but the taxi driver just smiled and waved his hand.

The man asked the driver how he could be so calm and relaxed, and so friendly when the other guy almost ruined his car and was so angry…

The taxi driver replied, People are like garbage trucks. They run around with garbage, full of disappointment, full of anger, and when the garbage piles up, they need a place to dump it on, and sometimes they dump it on you.

But you don't take it personally, just wave, smile, you wish them well, and move on."

Don't let that garbage spread to other people at work, or at home, or on the streets… you love those who treat you right and pray for those who don't. Life is 10% of what you make it, and the other 90% is how you take it.

The Pastor's Ass

A pastor entered his donkey in a race, and it won…The pastor was so pleased with the donkey that he entered it in the race again, and it won again... The local paper read, PASTOR'S ASS OUT FRONT.

The bishop was so upset with this kind of publicity that he ordered the Pastor not to enter the donkey in another race... The next day the local paper headline read, BISHOP SCRATCHES PASTOR'S ASS.

This was too much for the bishop so he ordered the pastor to get rid of the donkey. The pastor decided to give it to a nun in a nearby convent and ... the local paper, hearing of the news, posted the following headline the next day, NUN HAS BEST ASS IN TOWN.

The bishop fainted, and he informed the nun that she would have to get rid of the donkey, so she sold it to a farm for £10. The next day the paper read, NUN SELLS ASS FOR £10.

This was too much for the bishop, so he ordered the nun to buy back the donkey and lead it to the plains where it could run wild. The next day the headlines read, NUN ANNOUNCES HER ASS IS WILD AND FREE.

The bishop was buried the next day.

The moral of the story is that being concerned about public opinion can bring you much grief and misery and even shortens your life, so be yourself and enjoy life, stop worrying about everyone else's ass, and just cover your own! You will be a lot happier and live longer.

Another area where we can get stressed about things is, when we have differences of opinions with other people, because maybe they don't think the same way we do. A practical demonstration I normally do in my workshops and the motivational shows is this one:-

Empathy

I get a half-white-/-half-black ball, and get two volunteers to come up and look away from the ball. I then get them to turn around and I ask what colour the ball is.

Then without looking at the ball, I ask them to switch places, and turn around again, and ask them again what colour the ball is, of course, it is different this time.

Throughout our lives, we believe many things, which we hold dear, and what we think is right.

There will be times when others will disagree with us, what we think and believe is 100% right, but they believe the opposite just as strongly. How can that be? Can't they see?

We can be frustrated, we might grow distant, we might even sever relationships. SLOW DOWN… breathe… and STEP INTO THE OTHER PERSON'S SHOES. It will make a difference.

The stress glass

How heavy is a glass of water? The absolute weight of the glass of water doesn't matter, it depends on how long you hold onto it.

If you hold it for a minute, nothing happens.

If you hold it for an hour, your arm will begin to ache.

If you hold it for a day, your arm will feel numb and paralysed.

The weight of the glass hasn't changed, but the longer you hold onto it, the heavier it becomes.

The stresses and worries of life are like this glass of water. If you think about them for a little while there is no problem.

If you think about them for a bit longer it begins to hurt.

If you think about them all day long, you will feel paralysed and incapable of doing anything.

Always remember to put the glass down!

Chapter 2
Mental Health

I have had many years of experience in the Mental Health area, and have also worked at a number of Mental Health Hospitals and seen a lot of things in my time. But let's explore Mental Health in more detail.

"Mental health is not just the absence of disease or illness, it is a positive state of mind which allows an individual to do more than just cope with life, it enables continual growth and the fulfilment of potential."

People can suffer from a lot of problems which affect their mental health in a variety of ways, some of which can be quite mild and can be managed quite easily, and others, where they are affected quite badly every-day.

Depression
We all have times in our life where we sometimes feel happy, and at other times sad. It is normal to feel down when we are ill, or suffer a break-up or suffer a loss, it is a normal reaction. Although we might describe ourselves as feeling 'depressed 'in these situations, this isn't depression in a clinical sense.

I want to go through this in a little detail, as this could help you with someone you know in the future, and even yourself.

Depression in a clinical sense is when you have a low mood, but one that continues for at least two weeks. Whilst many of us can feel sad when things aren't right, we often improve quickly, but a person with depression can remain in a very low mood for months and even years. Other signs that someone is really depressed are losing interest and enjoyment in the things they used to like doing.

You may find people with depression have a general lack of energy and zest for life, and feeling lonely and isolated, and things like low appetite.

"It is difficult to describe depression to someone who's never been there because it's not sadness. Sadness is to cry and to feel. But it's that cold absence of feeling – that really hollowed-out feeling." J.K. Rowling

Depression is more than just feeling 'down'. It is losing that desire, that interest in day to day life and having no interest in life in general.

Anxiety

There are different types of anxiety, including Generalised Anxiety Disorder (GAD), phobic disorder and also PTSD (Post Traumatic Stress Disorder).

Anxiety and Depression can affects someone's normal life quite significantly and the activities they do day to day. Anxiety can make meeting new people a nightmare, and anxiety disorder is a feeling of fear and worry that is severe and long-lasting.

With Generalised Anxiety Disorder, its not like having anxiety over a job interview, or a test, which we all feel, it is more of a constant worry, or worry attached to a specific event, and often it is brought on by situations a person perceives as threatening, or from being in an environment where you feel you don't have any control over. This feeling is part of the stress 'fight or flight' response.

Bipolar

With Bipolar, there are two extremes, one being depression. Where there are feelings of sadness, hopelessness, and sometimes not wanting to live anymore. Depression is what they call a Unipolar experience, which means there is just one side to it.

With Bipolar it is more like a seesaw... At one end of the scale is depression, and at the other is quite the opposite in Mania.

The individual can spend much time either in deep depression, or on the manic high of mania. They can go from the extreme of depression, to somewhere in the middle, to the manic phase.

Because the timings of depression and mania vary, Bipolar can be very difficult to diagnose because both sides have to be present.

Psychosis
Psychosis possibly carries the largest stigma within all of the mental Health conditions. This maybe due to the fact that people here the word psychosis and link it to the word 'psycho', which is actually an abbreviation of psychopathy, which is totally different as this is where a person has reduced concern and care for others, has criminal tendencies and lacks remorse. So, when someone refers to someone with psychosis as a 'psycho 'this is not only inaccurate but also very hurtful also.

So what is psychosis? In reality it is a general term to describe conditions where the person's perception of reality is different than what is agreed upon by others.

One symptom of psychosis is having auditory hallucinations (hearing voices). The problem is for the individual with psychosis, the voices are very real.

Other symptoms include, thought disturbances, delusions and auditory hallucinations.

The thought disturbances can appear in several forms, which are:-

- Thought insertion:- which is the belief that your thoughts are not your own, and have been placed there by outside forces, i.e. aliens, etc.
- thought withdrawal, is the belief that your thoughts are being taken from you, also by outside forces.
- Thought broadcasting is where the person thinks that their thoughts are being made known to others, this could include the government, aliens, communists, or other relevant organisations.

When a person suffers with auditory hallucinations, they experience hearing these other voices that nobody else can hear, and these voices are usually giving a negative, hurtful running commentary of the person's life and often using upsetting and obscene language. These voices might try to persuade the person to commit violent acts and crimes. What really is important to realise, is that for the individual, the voices don't come from within, but really are actually something that is being heard.

These voices relate to a delusion that the person is currently experiencing, reinforcing the 'reality 'of their faulty belief.

With delusions, the person with psychosis believes the false beliefs to be true, despite any evidence to the contrary. Someone with psychosis could have delusions of grandeur, where they believe themselves to be a famous or important person. It could also show where they believe they have increased abilities and intelligence.

A person who has paranoid delusions can believe that they are being persecuted in some way, for example, aliens watching them, or they are being followed or watched.

They may also believe that they are deliberately being tricked, ridiculed or tormented.

Sometimes the person may believe that there is something wrong with their physical health which is called a somatic delusion. These delusions feel real to the person, even when they are shown evidence that they are wrong,

So, in conclusion, psychosis is losing touch with reality in some way. Mental health conditions such as bipolar, psychotic depression, substance abuse, and schizoaffective disorder can all be seen as conditions that can have symptoms of psychosis.

<u>Phobias</u>
There are 3 accepted categories of phobias.
1. Specific phobias
2. Social phobias
3. Agoraphobia

Specific phobias normally focus on one thing that is the source of the person's anxiety. These could be, cynophobia, which is having a fear of dogs, or Arachnophobia, which is a fear of spiders, or claustrophobia, which is the fear of enclosed spaces, but the interesting thing is, that almost anything has the potential to cause a phobic reaction.

Sometimes the source of the phobia can seem reasonable to others, such as a fear of disease which is pathophobia. But with other phobias, it is hard to understand why the phobia is so powerful when it seems so irrational.

The important thing to remember though is that the feeling of fear is very real for the person experiencing it. Part of the definition of a phobia is that it is irrational, but this is difficult to convince a person that the fear isn't really dangerous or frightening.

What sometimes happens is that the person then tries to avoid the source of fear, and this can become a dominating force in that person's life, and this can affect the person's quality of life, and even disrupt their everyday functioning.

Phobias usually develop in childhood, but they can appear later in life too.

Social phobias are known as complex phobias. Generally, the feeling in these cases is that the person will embarrass or humiliate themselves in front of other people. Social phobias can make people experience a high level of anxiety in situations that most of us would not find at all threatening.

Things that most of us find so easy to do and so natural such as writing when someone is watching, or eating and drinking in front of others could cause great anxiety to someone who has this phobia. Unfortunately, this can become time-consuming, and life-disrupting if the person starts avoiding social situations. They could find working with others very difficult, because they feel that fear of being humiliated and being embarrassed.

With Agoraphobia, this is a fear of being in a situation where help is not nearby if something happens. It is being away from home, or a safe space. A person who suffers from Agoraphobia may be very afraid to leave their home in case they are attacked, as it is also a fear of being unable to escape a dangerous situation.

Eating disorders

The two main eating disorders are Bulimia and Anorexia. Anorexia is an attempt by a person to reduce their body weight, by taking in an inadequate amount of food, and also by behaviours such as purging which includes vomiting, excessive exercise and taking laxatives.

Bulimia, may have the same root cause as anorexia, but a person with bulimia may engage in periods of 'binge' eating and consume more than they need to feel full, and they try and remove this food from their system to avoid gaining weight, with similar purges as anorexia such as vomiting, laxatives and not eating for long periods.

Both of these conditions can cause serious harm to a person and can lead to severe illness and even death.

Schizophrenia

This is a condition that causes a range of psychological symptoms which includes hallucinations and delusions. Someone with schizophrenia may see, hear or believe things that seem and feel real to them but are not real to others around them. Symptoms of schizophrenia include hearing voices, seeing things that aren't real, unusual beliefs and confused thinking.

Schizoaffective disorder

Schizoaffective disorder is a mental illness that affects a person's mood, behaviour and thoughts, and may have symptoms of bipolar disorder and schizophrenia, including depression, psychosis and mania. Research has shown that about one in two hundred people may develop schizoaffective disorder at some point during their life.

Self- Harm

Self- harm is where somebody repeatedly and intentionally harms themselves, in a way that is not intended to be lethal and is impulsive. The most common methods are skin cutting, head banging or hitting, burning, ligatures, excessive scratching, and punching objects. Research indicates that self-harm affects as many as 4% of adults in European countries.

These rates are higher among adolescents. People who self-harm often report that they feel empty inside, under-stimulated, unable to express their feelings, feeling lonely and not understood by others.

Self-harm is for many their way to cope with painful or hard to express feelings, or a way that someone has control over their body when they can't control anything else in their life. and often a self-destructive cycle often develops without proper treatment.

Suicidal tendencies

This may be difficult for many people to understand why someone would want to take their own life, but for the suicidal person they may be in so much pain that the person can see no other option. Suicide is the 2nd leading cause of death between 15-29 year olds.

Most suicidal individuals will display warning signs of their intentions to commit suicide. Some of these warning signs include:-

- Loss of energy
- Changes to sleeping patterns
- Loss of interest in personal hygiene or appearance
- Loss of interest in sex
- Weight gain or loss
- Extreme changes in eating habits, either loss of appetite or increase in appetite.

You may notice signs in how they talk and behave, such as
- saying things like' there is no future'
- feelings of guilt
- they want to escape
- feeling alone and helplessness
- talking about suicide or death
- planning for suicide
- withdrawal from family and friends
- alcohol or drug misuse
- abandoning activities which were previously important.
- Self-harming
- Putting affairs in order
- Risk taking or recklessness
- Unexplained crying
- Emotional outburst

- Sadness, anger, disconnection, worthlessness, loneliness and isolation

There are many reasons why someone could develop mental health issues, including biological causes such as chemical imbalances, trauma, stress, grief and bereavement, bullying and cyber bullying etc.

Mental health in the Workplace.

What I would like to cover in a little detail in this book is Mental health in the workplace.

I think in some places, the mental health of employees, and colleagues is sometimes overlooked.

Did you know that looking after your staff who work for you can actually save you time, energy and money. When you look after your team, it is actually easier to hit targets because employees become more productive.

Being proactive about the mental health of your team will also, reduce conflict and reduce employee absence. It also makes your team more efficient and more resilient.

Poor mental health at work affects people, businesses and the economy. In recent years a number of studies have worked out the cost of these issues...

How much do you think the cost is?

It is actually Billions!!

A study in the UK done by Deloitte (2020) puts the cost to businesses at.... £40 Billion to £45 Billion. And the cost to society as a whole at £99 Billion.

Poor mental health is extremely expensive. The costs for the business comes from a range of places such as turnover, absenteeism, and presenteeism.

Absenteeism costs around £8 Billion,

Presenteeism, where people turn up but are not effective, the cost is between £17 Billion to £26 billion.

Turnover is approximately £8 Billion

Investing in mental health is really good for business. For every £1 invested, what do you think the return of investment (ROI) is?

The ROI is actually £5 in the latest study from Deloitte for well-being support.

Here is the breakdown of the ROI's of the types and stages on intervention.
- Reactive 1 to 1 support:- counselling, psychotherapy and employee assistance programs... the ROI is 5:1
- Proactive support:- Mental health workshops, health and wellbeing coaching... the ROI is 6:1
- Cultural change and raising awareness... the ROI is 8:1

The Human cost for poor mental health comes up with quite shocking figures... You have to remember, people are really affected by the conditions they have, and you can make a real difference.
- 1 in 4 people will have a common mental disorder at some point in their lives (NHS 2014)
- 75% of those with a diagnosable mental health disorder receive no treatment at all (Davies, 2014)
- 57% of people would not feel able to disclose a mental health condition they were suffering from to anyone else (Capita, 2015)
- Every year 300,000 people with long term mental health condition lose their jobs (labour force survey (2016-17)
- Somewhere in the world a suicide takes place every 40 seconds (NHS 2014)
- For every 1 suicide, there are 25 attempts (international association for suicide prevention) (2017)
- Men are 3 times more likely to commit suicide than women (NHS 2014)
- 36% of employees have complained to their employer about stress in the past, but the employer has done nothing to help (Capita 2017)
- 49% of work related abscences are due to stress, anxiety or depression (labour force survey 2017)
- 90% of employees would not feel comfortable disclosing a mental health condition to their line manager (Business in the community 2017)

One of the most difficult things for someone with mental health problems, is having to hide it from people. There is a lot of stigma around still about mental health issues unfortunately.

There are four steps to tackle the stigma and prevent a snowball effect:-
1. Acknowledge negative feelings
2. De-medicalise mental health
3. Recognise mental health as a continuum.
4. Appreciate the link between mental health, presenteeism and productivity.

Mental health, depression and stress are all major problems in modern life. Even the strongest hands can lose their grip, the greatest minds can become cloudy, and the biggest hearts can break... so please BE KIND always.

So many people are hanging on by the thinnest of threads... treat people well... you could just be that thread.

Your mental health is more important than the test, the interview, the lunch date, the meeting, the family dinner, the football game, the recital or the grocery run. Take care of yourself.

I want to share a poem with you which may resonate with some people who are struggling with depression and their mental health.

<u>The mountain</u>

If the mountain seems too big today, then climb a hill instead... If the morning brings you sadness, it's ok to stay in bed

If the day ahead weighs heavy, and your plans feel like a curse.... There's no shame in rearranging, don't make yourself feel worse

If a shower stings like needles, and a bath feels like you'll drown... If you haven't washed your hair for days, don't throw away your crown

A day is not a lifetime, a rest is not defeat... Don't think of it as failure, just a quiet kind retreat

It's ok to take a moment, from an anxious fractured mind...
The world will not stop turning, while you get yourself realigned
The mountain will still be there, when you want to try again...
You can climb it in your own time, just love yourself 'till then

Be gentle with the people you meet, their outsides may not match their insides.
"You know i think childhood is where you idolise Batman, but in adulthood, you maybe realise the Joker makes more sense"
Just remember, every situation in life is TEMPORARY, so when life is good, make sure you enjoy and receive it fully. When life is not so good, remember that it WILL NOT last forever, and better days are on the way.
I want to share another poem which was written by an incredible young lady still at school, it's for anyone struggling with their mental health, and trying to turn those negative feelings around. It is called the reverse poem:-

I don't deserve to be alive...and i refuse to believe that...
I have a purpose on this earth....
It's no shock that...i am amazing... is a lie
I am a failure... i have issues
I do not conclude that... life is worth living
Now and forever.... my world will be miserable
I will no longer think that.... there is still hope
I know.... i am ready to end my life
Never again will i say that... it is getting better

And the reverse
It IS getting better
Never again will i say that... i am ready to end my life
I know... there is still hope
I will no longer think that... my world will be miserable
Now and forever... life is worth living
I do not conclude that... i have issues
I am a failure... is a lie.. I am amazing
It's no shock that... i have a purpose on this earth
And i refuse to believe that.. I don't deserve to be alive.

The things that you need to focus on in life are your loved ones, how far you have come, finding time for yourself, your happiness, staying healthy, loving yourself. Stay strong, and when life gives you a 100 reasons to break down and cry, show life that you have a million reasons to smile and laugh.

The ALRIGHT Method

This is a tried and tested way to have conversations with family, friends, people around you and colleagues at work etc. If someone doesn't seem to be themselves, they seem stressed, tearful and they don't seem themselves. Here is a method which can help you connect with people you may feel are struggling.

APPROACH:- Approach the person, in a warm friendly manner, asking how the person is doing etc.

LISTEN:- if they open up to you about an issue they have, listen to them, let them talk, be interested, use silence, give undivided attention, don't judge, LISTEN!

REASSURE:- After opening up to you, they may be feeling very vulnerable, so you need to reassure them, you don't need to be an expert, don't try to give reasons why they feel the way they do. Let them know they are valued, explain you will do what you can do to help, give them a sense of hope.

IMMEDIATE ACTIONS:- consider anything you might need to do straight away. They may be feeling quite emotional so give them some time. Ask them if they need any support (especially if in work setting), show that you are there to support them.

GUIDE towards professional support:- Professional support could come from their doctor, counselling, local support groups, community mental health treatments.

HELP them help themselves:- such as exercise, relaxation and meditation, research self-help, engage with family and friends, and engage in fulfilling activities.

TIME:- make time to organise another chat or meeting with them, to catch up with them to see if they are feeling any better.

As an alternative therapist and master hypnotist, I am not going to advocate medications for mental health. Although they are effective in masking the symptoms, and helping people cope with their mental health issues, it is not dealing with the issues causing the mental health problems, be it chemical imbalances and deficiencies, trauma, stress etc.

If a person has been abused, raped, been badly bullied, or had an awful childhood which affected their mental health, it doesn't matter how many drugs you give them to numb out that pain, or how many coping skills you give them through counselling and talk therapies, they are still left feeling that original traumatic event or trauma. You are basically just putting a plaster over something which needs fixing at a deeper level.

During my time working in Mental Health, I have seen many hundreds of people with Mental Health issues, all of them on medication to help block out these feelings.

All medications come with side effects, but these people will always feel this way, and will not be able to have any sort of meaningful life, and will be in and out of mental health hospitals their whole life, because the actual problem is never actually dealt with, it is just masked.

It is very much like the asthmatic who is given an inhaler stop the wheezing, and to mask the problem. Yes it stops an asthma attack, but it never actually deals with why that person is having those attacks in the first place.

I have sat in a room talking to a patient, who is self-harming, and also breaking down crying and on different medications, but still crying out for help to deal with the issues actually causing their mental health in the first place, the trauma, and the original events which are playing in their head constantly.

As a therapist, and more specifically an hypnotherapist and trauma specialist, I am available to help people who are suffering from trauma, addiction and mental health problems, and I would strongly advise anybody who is suffering in this way to speak to a therapist to release trauma, and help deal with issues.

When trauma has caused mental health problems, although talk therapies can help with coping skills etc, they don't actually deal with the trauma etc causing the mental health issues. The trauma which causes these issues is in the subconscious mind, and the only way of releasing trauma, fears, phobias, addictions is through therapies such as Hypnosis, Neuro Lingual

Programming, EMDR, narrative exposure therapy and timeline therapy, as they deal with releasing the problems, or the feeling associated with the problem.

Giving medication is just masking problems and not actually dealing with the underlying issues.

For the pharmaceutical companies it is wonderful as they have patients for life, but for the actual patient, they are stuck in 'groundhog day 'where they cannot move on with life, they can't get their life back on track, and many will spend years in and out of hospital, or zonked out with the side effects of the medication they are put on.

The Viking Buddha has another book due out by the end of 2024, which is called, 'Calm amidst the Storm' and it is a comprehensive guide for families and loved ones, and goes into much more detail about mental health issues and challenges and how to support people with mental health problems.

Chapter 3
Alcohol & Substance Abuse

I started working for the NHS, and more specifically for Blackpool Hospital in 2011. My first job there was on the Gastro Ward, which I can tell you was an eye opening experience. Most of the problem patients, the one's who were withdrawing from their high of substances or alcohol, were put on there, and it first opened my eyes to the absolute destruction alcohol and drugs actually does to people. It has to be said, we had the best team on there, but it had to be, as it was a very difficult place at times.

I have seen patients sat up in beds telling me to get away, as they were driving their car. The paranoia, and also the other end of the scale, where after years of abusing their bodies with alcohol, the liver finally gives in, it isn't working anymore, the have ascites, where the fluid goes into the stomach and it has to be drained, and they have jaundice, and the amount of times that I had the conversation with patients who had got to that heartbreaking stage, the regrets they had, how they wish they had changed sooner, and not drank themselves to an early death.

I went on to spend a few more years working with substance abuse and alcohol as a support worker, and alcohol really is a killer alongside substances and drugs.

So, I want to go a little more into the destructive properties of alcohol, and how it can and does destroy so many lives.

So what is addiction

"Addiction is a condition that results when a person ingests a substance, ie, alcohol, cocaine, nicotine, or engages in an activity such as gambling, sex, shopping, that can be pleasurable, but the continuation of which becomes compulsive and interferes with ordinary responsibilities and concerns such as work, relationships or health"

Addiction is a complex condition, a brain disease, that is manifested by compulsive substance use despite harmful consequence. People with addiction have an intense focus on using a certain substance, such as alcohol, or drugs, to the point that it takes over their life. They keep using alcohol or a drug even when they know it will cause problems.

So what is a drug? The World Health Organisation defines a drug as anything other than food or water, that alters the function of the mind or body.

There are 4 phases of addiction

1. Experimental:- learns that experimenting with the substance makes one feel good. The person doesn't recognise any serious negative consequences, learns to trust the drug and also learns how much to use to feel good.

2. Social:- They use more, and make this a part of social life, and they try and make safe rules for themselves regarding the use, and it turns into a problem without warning.

3. Daily Preoccupation (Harmful dependency):- this is where it becomes a harmful dependency, and they begin to lose control over the use of the substance, cannot block out the emotional pain, and unresolved problems produce more stress and pain, their lifestyle centres on compulsive behaviour and their self-imposed rules are broken regularly. This affects their health, emotions, relationships and spirituality.

4. Using to feel normal (full blown addiction):- snowball effect, loss of control and dignity, broken family relationships, paranoid thinking and delusion, sometimes no desire to live

The interventions we can use for the different phases are as follows:-

1. Experimentation:- drug information, education, and harm minimisation

2. Social:- give the person education, drug information, counselling and harm minimisation

3. Harmful dependency:- support groups, medical support, detox, counselling, rehab

4. Addiction:- medical support, group support, counselling, rehab, detox

Stages of change
1. Pre-contemplative:- they haven't considered they have alcohol / drug problem, therefore they are not thinking about changing the usage and patterns
2. Contemplative:- this is where they have identified they have a problem, and they are thinking about making changes. However no change occurs
3. Decision:- this is where they know they have a alcohol / drug problem and they are planning to do something about it.
4. Action:- treatment starts, and the drug/alcohol use declines and stops.
5. Maintenance:- this is where they have ongoing treatment, and find strategies to prevent a relapse, and monitor the progress.

Alcohol
Alcohol is a drug! Alcohol enters the blood stream and brain rapidly from the stomach. What alcohol does is, that it targets the brain chemicals just like other drugs.
Alcohol slows down the messages going to and from the brain by depressing the brains activity.
It is a fact that females are more affected by alcohol than males, because alcohol is broken down by the liver, and females have smaller livers than males, and also females produce less dehydrogenase which is an enzyme that breaks down alcohol.
If someone is pregnant and they drink alcohol, the alcohol passes straight to the baby via the placenta. So if the mother is drunk, then the baby is too.
The alcohol affects on children and adolescents are that children and adolescents absorb alcohol faster, and their livers metabolise alcohol less efficiently, and the three leading causes of death amongst adolescents are unintentional injury, suicide and homicide, and these are all associated with alcohol.

Binge drinking
When someone goes out and indulges in binge drinking, this can lead to alcohol poisoning. Alcohol poisoning is where blood alcohol levels rise to such dangerous level, and shuts down

critical organs, causing loss of consciousness, and slowing the heart beat and breathing. People can die from too much alcohol.

Symptoms of alcohol poisoning are:- unable to wake up, their skin is pale, cold, blue or purplish, their breathing is very slow, vomiting without waking up, conscious and vomiting a lot, and someone can die while they are quietly sleeping it off in the corner.

Cannabis

Cannabis is a drug. It contains over 420 chemicals, and when combusted contains over 2000 chemicals. There isn't another illicit drug that is found to have all these chemical properties.

Cannabis actually acts on certain specific areas in the human brain called cannabinoid receptors, which normally receive our own cannabis type chemicals called anandamide, which is the human brain cannabinoid. THC from the cannabis targets cannabinoid receptors and it interferes with normal brain functioning.

The use of cannabis is associated with greater psychotic symptoms, increased risk of aggression, and increased delusional ideas.

Amphetamines

Amphetamines are drugs that stimulate brain activity. And they speed up messages going to and from the brain, such as speed, whiz, uppers, and ice.

Methylamphetamines such as ICE and Crystalline Methylamphetamine can be fatal. The effects on the body usually last about 4-6 hours, however it can be up to 36 hours.

The effects of amphetamines and ecstasy, are that it causes large amounts of chemicals such as adrenaline, noradrenaline, serotonin and dopamine to be released in the brain. These chemicals regulate our emotions such as depression / anxiety, our mood (happy/aggressive), BP, Heart rate, temperature, airways and pain perception.

Symptoms of amphetamine use are
- Racing pulse / chest pain
- Rapid breathing / fainting

- Large pupils, nausea, vomiting
- Increased blood pressure and headaches
- Sweating – hot and high temperature
- Overconfidence, hyper alert, easily startled
- Anxious, confused, increased agitation

Other behavioural signs could be aggression, violent outbursts, extra strength, psychosis, paranoia, delusions, and out of touch with reality. There is also an increased risk of suicide.

Some common ingredients in ICE are acetone, lithium, toluene, hydrochloric acid, pseudoephedrine, red phosphorus, sodium hydroxide sulfuric acid and anhydrous ammonia

Ecstasy

Ecstasy (methylene-dioxy-meth-amphetamine) MDMA, which is also called the love drug and dance drug, is a brain stimulant, and yes, one pill could kill you.

The effects of ecstasy lasts about 3 to 4 hours, and peaks in about 2 hours. The signs of ecstasy include large pupils, headaches, increased BP, nausea and vomiting, teeth grinding, jaw clenching, dry mouth, sweating with body temperature rising. There can also be rapid breathing, and uncontrollable movement in limbs. There is a feeling well-being, increased closeness to others, lack of inhibitions, increased confidence and inability to sleep. Other signs could be anxiety, psychosis, paranoia

Inhalants

These are chemicals that give off fumes which cause intoxication and have mind altering qualities, such as glues, paints, petrol, lighter fuel, hair sprays, nail polish removers, air fresheners, deodorants etc.

The side effects and symptoms include drowsiness, slurred speech, confusion, disorientation, irritability and agitation, sneezing, coughing, blood shot eyes, nose bleeds, large pupils and chest pain and of course death.

It can cause convulsions, unconsciousness, breathing depression, heart failure, bronchospasms, and lethal heart rhythms.

Cocaine

Cocaine comes in the form of powder, and gives the user a short lived high which works by speeding up your mind. When cocaine is mixed with alcohol, they interact producing a toxic chemical called Cocethylene which is very dangerous.

Heroin

And finally.... Heroin which is a natural opiate that is made from morphine. This gives the user a feeling of warmth, well-being, sleepy and relaxed. The effects are respiratory failure, coma, death, and of course is highly addictive.

Of course, to live the best life you can do, which is what this book is ultimately about, ridding yourself from all of these toxins, and getting the help you need and the support you need if you are suffering from addiction, is so important. It is important to clean your life up, as all of these substances are toxic, they ruin your life and stop you from reaching your full potential.

Smoking

Now this certain area is one of the areas which kind of get me a little vexed, more for the big notices on a packet of cigarettes stating "Cigarettes Cause Cancer".

Yes of course they are carcinogenic, and can contribute to you developing cancer, but if cigarettes have a notice on saying these will kill you and cause cancer, so should alcohol, processed foods, cakes, MEAT, sweets, and most takeaways.

All of the above are not good for you, carcinogenic, and over time may well lead to cancer. But it just simply isn't true that smoking will give you cancer on its own. If that was the case, why does a man who has been smoking thirty cigarettes a day for the last forty years not have cancer?

Not that I am advocating smoking, as it is from a common-sense point of view alone, a stupid thing to do. It doesn't really take a genius to realise that inhaling smoke into your mouth and lungs, which is full of poisons, it isn't the best thing you should be doing, and it really isn't going to help you live to 100 year old is it.

Smoking is very bad for your health of course, as is vaping. Unfortunately, many people now vape instead, thinking that is somehow safe, and not bad for your health. Vaping is not good for your health either, and there have been reports that this may cause pockets in your lungs.

So, let's look at smoking in a little closer detail.

What happens when you smoke?
- Within 10 seconds of taking your first drag, nicotine droplets are absorbed through the soft tissues of the mouth and throat.
- Within 10-19 seconds, the nicotine begins affecting the brain, causing the release of adrenaline. Adrenaline is a hormone that the body normally releases at times of stress, to put you on high alert, ready to stand your ground and fight or flight from danger.
- Within 1 minute of taking that first drag, adrenaline causes your heart to beat faster.
- Within ten minutes, the rate can rise as much as 30%. Can you feel this effect? Some smokers refer to this as the BUZZ.
- Meanwhile in your lungs, carbon monoxide is replacing oxygen. The red blood cells that normally carry oxygen from the lungs around your blood stream begin to carry carbon monoxide instead, making you feel dizzy and lightheaded. When you get this affect you are suffering from temporary oxygen starvation, which causes your nervous system to go into a mild spasm.
- You may feel a slight tingling in your fingers and toes, as they are not getting the oxygen they need.

We have seen that nicotine has a stimulant effect, triggering the body's stress response, but it is one of the many paradoxes of the chemical, as it can also have a sedative effect in larger doses, and over time.
- High doses of nicotine will poison you, causing nausea, vomiting, convulsions and even death. Just 60mg of nicotine on the tongue would kill a grown man.

All smokers are familiar with the nausea, and jangled nerves after they have smoked too much, and these are the symptoms of nicotine poisoning.

- The heightened physiological responses last for as long as you are smoking, and begin to decrease gradually for some hours afterwards, until the nicotine leaves your system or is topped up again.
- Within 1-2 hours of smoking their last cigarette, smokers will begin to experience physical symptoms attributable to the absence of nicotine. Their heart rate decreases, they feel anxious and stressed, and they experience cravings for more nicotine, which are relieved when they light their next cigarette.

The relief they feel on lighting up after a period without, leads many smokers to believe that smoking helps them to deal with stress... WRONG... it is smoking that has caused the stress in the first place by triggering adrenaline.

So what is in a cigarette?

Did you think it was just chopped up tobacco leaves in a paper tube? Cigarettes contain over 600 additives including:-

- Acetone, Benzene, Pyrene, Methanol, Nicotine, cadmium, Carbon Monoxide, Vinyl Chloride, Acid, Ammoniac, Arsenic, Polonium 210, DDT, Butane, Lead, and of course sugars, honey and chocolate to make it more addictive.

When these set on fire, the smoke contains over 4,000 chemicals, of which 50 are known to be carcinogenic, cancer forming, and dangerous. Which include:-

- Nicotine, arsenic, cyanide, Benzopyrene, ammonia, carbon monoxide, polonium 210, and Formaldehyde.

So, if you smoke, which one of these do you fancy? Take a pick, this is what a smoker is at risk of:-

- Aneurisms, angina, asthma, atherosclerosis, back pain, bronchitis, Cervical Cancer, cataracts, COPD, crohns Disease, depression, diabetes, duodenal ulcers, early menopause, emphysema, erectile dysfunction, gum disease,

- heart disease, impotence, infertility, intestinal polyps, kidney and bladder cancer, leukaemia, liver cancer, lung cancer, mouth and throat cancers, miscarriage, neck pain, pancreatic cancer, premature aging, stroke, stomach cancer, and much more.

What happens when you stop smoking?
- within twenty minutes you blood pressure and pulse return to normal.
- 8 hours, the nicotine and carbon monoxide in your blood reduced by half. Oxygen levels in blood return to normal.
- 24 hours, the carbon monoxide is expelled from the body, and the lungs start to clear out the tar encrusted mucus.
- 48 hours after stopping, all the nicotine has been expelled from the body, and there is significant improvement in skin pallor.
- 72 hours, and Your breathing is easier, as your bronchial tubes relax. Your energy levels increase.
- 1-2 weeks, and your concentration levels return to that of a non-smoker.
- 3-4 weeks, you may feel more cheerful as dopamine release systems get back to normal.
- 2-12 weeks, circulation is gradually improving
- 3-9 months, lung function improves by up to 10%
- 1 year, risk of heart attack falls to half that of a smoker.
- 5 years, risk of heart attack is almost as low as someone who has never smoked.
- 10 years, risk of lung cancer is half that of a smoker.

So, how much does your habit cost you?
On the next page there is a table, which is based on the average price of a pack of 20 cigarettes, and based on the price of £5 only. It shows how much people actually spend on cigarettes over a year, and what they will end up spending over a 20 year period.

	5 a day	10 day	20 day	30 day
week	£26.25	£52.50	£105	£157.50
month	£105	£210	£420	£630
1 year	£1,365	£2,730	£5,460	£8,190
5 years	£6,825	£13,650	£27,300	£40,950
10 years	£13,650	£27,300	£54,600	£81,900
20 years	£27,300	£54,600	£109,200	£163,800
30 years	£40,950	£81,900	£163,800	£245,700

If you are smoking 20 cigarettes a day over a year, that's £5,460 per year. That is one hell of a nice vacation right there isn't it?

And just thinking about the damage every single cigarette does to your body, and how long it takes your body to recover, I want to show how many cigarettes you are smoking over a year and longer. Have a look at the table on the next page, and it is a real eye opener to realise just how many of these toxic cigarettes you will put in your mouth over the years, and the amount of damage you are doing to your lungs and your body.

	5 day	10 day	20 day	30 day
1 week	35	70	140	210
1 month	140	280	560	840
1 year	1820	3640	7280	10,920
5 years	9,100	18,200	36,400	54,600
10 years	18,200	36,400	72,800	109,200
20 years	36,400	72,800	145,600	218,400

| 30 years | 54,600 | 109,200 | 218,400 | 327,600 |

I am not going to go any more into the benefits of stopping smoking, and why someone should stop smoking, because looking at the figures above and also what a cigarette contains, in addition to the problems it causes with your health, if someone doesn't want to stop smoking, armed with all the knowledge above then I am quite sure they don't want to stop smoking.

But what if you do want to stop?

Well, if you have the willpower to stop that's amazing, and I am sure the NHS and other organisations have patches and allsorts of other gadgets they think will help you stop smoking

Of course I am being biased now being an hypnotist, but the best way to stop smoking is by accessing your Subconscious mind, where all your habits, addictions, fears & phobias, trauma are stored, and this is best way to deal with the problems above, with hypnosis.

There is a chapter on hypnosis later in the book, which explains what hypnosis really is and what it isn't, and there are other therapies which can help you to stop smoking, but if you want to stop for good, and in a lot less time, and save yourself money, then hypnotherapy is the best way to go.

Chapter 4
Narcissistic Abuse

As part of The Viking Buddha workshops and training, we run workshops about Narcissistic Abuse and the 'Time to go' Domestic Abuse program, which also includes self-defence sessions, inspired by a truly amazing lady called Elle Beyer from the USA and her 'Badass women program'.

The first thing we need to do when talking about Narcissism is differentiate between a Narcissist, and someone who has NPD (Narcissistic Personality Disorder).

NPD is a serious Mental health issue, affecting personal life and relationships of the individual diagnosed.

A Narcissist can be anyone we know. In the USA, 1 in 200 people can be diagnosed with NPD, however narcissistic behaviour is much more prevalent in males than females.

There are a number of red flags when it comes to narcissistic people.

1. Things develop too fast
2. Narcissists are self-centred, they need admiration from others, they talk about themselves all the time and their accomplishments, they are not interested in your story and divert back to themselves.
3. They have the victim story:- story of their childhood and previous relationships, and being a victim, they typically have no long-term friendships, very few friends, difficult relationships with parents, being abandoned in the past, they come across as charming and loving, but no good past experiences of relationships. It's everybody else's fault.
4. The blame game:- they never blame themselves, it is always someone else's fault.
5. Arrogance:- they are arrogant, they feel superior to other people, they can be rude and abusive. They blame others and talk negatively about others.

6. Control and manipulation:- this may not be seen until much later in a relationship. They want to control the person, check up on you frequently, make decisions for you, expecting you to be grateful for everything, they may also tell you what to wear, or to behave in a certain way.

They will try to control your environment and your relationships with others, because the less you feel supported by others around you, the less likely it is that you will ever leave them.

They try and manipulate your feelings, so you feel guilty if you do something they don't like, or guilty for things you haven't even actually done.

Narcissistic parents

You can spot the narcissism in parents in how they behave with their children

1. They live through their child:- they can be controlling, they make all the decisions, the child has very little choice, the child is expected to achieve certain goals

2. Not good enough:- they put down their child, the parents feels threatened by the child's success, nit picking, unreasonable judgement and criticism, and the invalidation of positive attitude and emotions

3. Inflated ego:- the parents boasts about own achievements, amplifying own achievements, boasting about child's achievements drawing their future as of someone special, rich, famous etc. feeling superior

4. Superficial family image:- portraying child as the smartest, photos on social media, displaying material possessions, talking about own accomplishments

5. Manipulation of children:- guilt trips, blaming child for their misfortunes, shaming and negative comparisons to others.

6. Overly involved where the child is constantly taking various classes and what they want them to do, or under involved where the child is ignored.

7. Emotional blackmail:- 'how can you leave me' threatening to cut child out, crying to get child to feel sorry for them and to turn against others,

"Narcissistic personality disorder involves a distorted self-image. Emotions can be unstable, and intense, and there is excessive concern with vanity, prestige, power and personal adequacy. There also tends to be a lack of empathy and exaggerated sense of superiority"
The Medical News Today 2018

Healthy relationship

An healthy relationship consists of trust, patience, communication, respect, and healthy boundaries. Failures in relationships result from trust issues, not being understood or listened to, and consistently crossing the other person's boundaries, and also abuse, control and manipulation.

According to statistics only 10% of marriages in the USA can be considered as 'healthy and happy '(Acevedo et al 2012)

Virtually every relationship can be improved. The main problems which occur in a relationship are where there are trust issues which are brought from previous relationships, or which are developed over time due to a partner lying, infidelity, abuse or betrayal.

If you feel the relationship makes you unhappy, less valued and less respected over time, then you are in an unhealthy relationship.

Arguments and disagreements happen in all relationships, but in an healthy relationship both partners learn to listen and understand each other's point of view.

With toxic relationships, you find partners are not allowed to have their own viewpoints, there are nasty verbal fights, recalling the past verbal and physical abuse, and feeling exhausted after arguments.

In an healthy relationship there should be patience, empathy, genuine interest in each other's lives and experiences, affection towards one another and the ability to compromise and make allowances.

There should be appreciation and gratitude towards each other, and allowing room for growth with each other, with mutual respect related to views, beliefs, respecting privacy and reciprocity, respecting each other's boundaries and resolving conflicts respectfully.

When dating a narcissist, they are masters at creating an image of themselves which is very different from reality, and often it is only after a person starts investing in the relationship that the narcissist starts revealing their true colours, and by this time it is normally too late, and the person is committed and already convinced that he/she is the problem and not the narcissist, and the person is trapped.

It is therefore very important to start to recognise the signs at the earliest stage possible to avoid getting into a toxic and highly damaging relationship with a narcissist.

I can tell you from first-hand experience how you start to lose yourself, and start to believe that you are the problem, and it is all your fault, when really they are playing games with your head. I have been in 3 narcissistic relationships, and unfortunately as empaths, you are more likely to attract these energy vampires, who prey on your energy and your loving nature as you have something that they can never be.

It not only breaks you, but it can take away your self-confidence and self-esteem, as they slowly open up to who they really are taking more control over you, and isolating you more and more, and you find yourself saying sorry for things that they start intentionally, and when you react they say you are not right in the head, and need help, and you find yourself apologising for things you didn't even do in the first place.

The problem with this is when you do finally get out of the relationship, you don't realise how hurt and broken they made you, and if you don't heal properly, you can affect any decent relationship you have in the future, due to being so hurt, and the inability to trust people.

Unfortunately, many people tend to attract these type of people one after the other, and they know how to drain your energy, and make you feel guilty for things you haven't done.

Another trait of narcissists is to deny the most basic of human needs of love, affection, sex and attention over a certain period of time, and then you find yourself begging for attention. When you eventually crack, and say something, they make you out to be the one in the wrong, and you are too needy, and you need help. This is called avoidant abuse, and it is where someone willingly withdraws affection with the specific goal to hurt your feelings, control you or punish you

Continuing with the narcissistic evaluation, the narcissistic person is Grandiose, where they will exaggerate their good qualities, deny their flaws, and expect you to admire them. They need to control, including making decisions, ie restaurants, music, clothing etc.

They don't have any interest in your opinions and your likes, and it will always go back to what they believe, what they want, and always refocusing on themselves.

Narcissists are Omnipotent, which means they have the attitude of knowing what they are talking about, and in a lot of cases they don't, they are always right, they will not welcome your views, and the will try and talk negatively about others.

Abuse

According to the US national Domestic Violence Hotline (2020)

- Every minute, 24 people become victims of rape, physical violence, or stalking by an intimate partner.
- Nearly 3 in 10 women (29%) and 1 in 10 men (10%) have experienced rape, physical violence or staking by their partner
- 1 in 4 women (24.3%) and 1 in 7 men (13.8%) have been victims of severe physical violence by an intimate partner.
- Nearly half of all women and men have experienced psychological aggression by their partner.

There are 6 different types of abuse
1. Physical abuse:- punching, hitting, slapping, kicking, strangling, or physically restraining a partner against their will, shaking, pushing,
2. biting, scratching, throwing an object, pulling hair, grabbing clothing, grabbing face to make you look at them, grabbing you to force you to stay.

3. Sexual Abuse:- rape, forced sexual acts, withholding or using sex as a weapon, criticising or saying not good enough, sex can be used for power and control and can include emotional aspects to it. Sexual abuse can also include, unwanted kissing or touching, unwanted rough or violent sexual activity, restricting someone's access to birth control, sexual contact with someone drunk or unconscious, threatening someone to have sex, forcing sex with someone else.

4. Verbal / emotional / psychological abuse such as shouting, blaming, humiliating, criticizing, threatening, belittling, controlling someone's life, controlling communication with friends and family, silent treatment, manipulating feelings of guilt and jealousy, name calling.

5. Mental abuse:- making you doubt own sanity, making victim feel confused, hiding objects, denying what they said previously, being called crazy and need help etc, withholding approval or affection as punishment, always claiming to be right, being unfaithful, ignoring feelings, playing mind games

6. Financial abuse:- controlling person using finances, refusing access to money, refusing for person to get a job, running into debt and putting the debt onto the victim

7. Cultural / identity:- lack of respect for culture, racial, religious or spiritual identity. Making fun of person's beliefs or interests.

Gaslighting

This is a form of psychological abuse where the abuser manipulates the victim into doubting their own sanity, through lying, projecting own issues onto the victim or denying what they said earlier. The victim actually feels a need to defend and justify things they haven't even done, and then the narcissist uses love and flattery after the abusive behaviour which makes the victim really confused.

They may call you crazy and tell others you are crazy. This happens in a slow way over time.

The signs you need to get out

The signs that you need to get out of this toxic relationship are:-
- You are not comfortable.
- You need to be careful what you say with certain things and topics.
- You are tense when you are with that person.
- You feel relaxed when they are not there.
- You blame yourself often.
- Your mental health is suffering.
- You don't like the way you feel.
- You cannot say that you are happy in this relationship.
- You are not getting emotional support, love, and appreciation.
- You keep saying nice things but get nothing back.
- You have changed but not in a good way.
- You are becoming more resentful, bitter, angry, frustrated, negative, and becoming more like them.
- You are in a constant state of stress.
- You are getting frequent headaches, allergies, skin issues. You feel trapped, helpless and unable to escape.
- You feel guilty, more confused, looking at other happy couples feeling sad.
- You are constantly counting reasons for staying v leaving. You are afraid of the person you are with. Abusive behaviour gets worse.

Trauma bonding is an unhealthy attachment created by emotional push and pull and is not healthy in a relationship.

Getting out of the toxic relationship

It is important to get support from others and find help:-
- From friends and family, Counselling, psychotherapy, helplines, DV groups, charitable organisations, forums, social media groups,

What is important, is that you take a no contact approach, unless there are children involved, or you have to negotiate divorce procedures. It is important that there is very little contact, because if you don't do this, they can reel you back in, and you can go back to this person, and you are under their control again.

The Viking Buddha runs workshops and groups at times throughout the year, which is for Narcissistic and Domestic Abuse victims.
Dates can be found on the website.
www.thevikingbuddha.com

Chapter 5
Bullying

So, why should we treat bullying so seriously?

What for some is good fun and a joke, for others it is distressful and harmful.

So, what is bullying? And how is it different from a simple disagreement?

Bullying is a form of violence, it is aimed at hurting another person, by arousing fear, causing distress, humiliating or causing physical pain. Bullying is never a random incident.

Bullying is fully intentional, it is done repeatedly, and aimed at causing anguish to the other person. The suffering is even greater, because these incidents are usually observed by a group of spectators, and the victim does not have any chance to defend themselves.

So, what is the difference between ordinary day to day misunderstandings then? It is the duration! Bullying is usually long lasting, and normally, there is the advantage the offender has over the victim, like age or strength.

So, what actions constitute to being bullying behaviour?

Direct Physical bullying is pushing, spitting, hitting, kicking, taking things from the victim, and being forced to do unwanted humiliating activities.

Emotional verbal bullying is humiliating, making fun of somebody, threatening and provoking them.

Indirect, concealed, relational bullying is backbiting, gossiping, and persuading others to isolate the victim. Basically, bullying is a behaviour that is aimed at hurting the other person, making them feel threatened and hounded, and being rejected by their peers.

Cyber-bullying:- According to various statistics, between 20% to 50% of young people suffer from Cyber-bullying. It is a very serious problem, which can result in devastating consequences. Suicide is one of the many devastating outcomes of cyber-bullying.

Virtual reality makes mental abuse easy to employ, as the offender often remains anonymous, and their actions, made public on the internet provide them with a wide audience. It is a form of aggression that does not take much effort, yet removing its results is extremely hard.

With Cyber-bullying, the main difference is the tool, where a mobile phone or laptop is used, and the content can go viral. This will hurt the person each time they see it, or when someone reminds him or her of it. It is harder for the offender to see the harm that they have caused, and without feelings of guilt, they will have no reason to stop acting in this manner.

The declaration against bullying in children and youth was signed in Switzerland in 2007. This document has emphasised the role and the responsibilities of adults, with the words "every child and youth, among other rights, has the right to be respected and safe, which is the moral and legal responsibility of adults"

It might seem that physical bullying is the most harmful and most dangerous, yet, this isn't true, as all forms of bullying are equally dangerous.

Verbal bullying undermines self-esteem, generates fear, and generates feelings of embarrassment, which have a long-lasting impact.

Relational bullying is the most harmful for the youth's self-esteem, as it includes being excluded from peer groups, by isolation, spreading gossip, not inviting him or her to parties, and this is hard to bear for a young person, especially at school age, when relationships with their peers is so important for the development of their identity.

Verbal and relational violence occur twice as often as physical bullying, but parents and teachers often don't manage to notice it. This type of bullying results in great damage to the victim, as long-lasting stress and poor mental health are connected with this type of bullying, which causes problems in future years for the victim.

Why are some people so engaged in hurting others online? Children who are allowed to use their mobile phones, laptops and computers with internet connection, quickly learn how to use them efficiently. They can use the tools, and understand the principles of the web far better than many adults.

Did you know that cyberbullying represents one of the main causes of depression and suicide among kids at school.

What is cyber-stalking? This is where a child follows someone on the internet for a long period of time, and disrupts their life, and communicates to them in a way that the victim is afraid of their peace and safety.

There is another term which is used, and this is called a flame war. This is where aggressive exchanges of views between several people happen, and it is usually conducted publicly in chat rooms or in discussion groups.

Another problem with cyber-bullying is harassment, where bullies send aggressive, disgraceful, insulting, and vulgar messages to the victim by electronic means of communication regularly.

Another particularly awful side of cyber-bullying is called outing, where bullies steal information from the victim's computer, or records of phone conversations, films and photos, and these can instantly be made publicly available.

Denigration is where the bullies publish fake information or materials about someone, often with altered films and photos suggesting the victim is performing sexual acts etc, which is highly distressing for the victims.

It is such a shame that the bullies can't see the damage they do, not just physically but emotionally. The victims who suffer from bullying and cyber-bullying, experience such emotions as embarrassment, anxiety, sadness, humiliation, and helplessness. The longer the violent behaviour lasts, the more intensive these emotions can become.

The consequences of bullying continue long after the bullying has stopped, and can influence the entire personality of the victims. In the future, the victims may well end up with low self-esteem, mental health problems, self-harming, eating disorders, and actually feel guilty themselves for all those unfortunate situations that happened to them.

The vast majority of children that suffered from bullying will have problems building relationships, as it causes some great dysfunctions, both when experiencing the bullying, and into their adolescent and adult life.

Victims find it difficult to talk about their problems, they will feel ashamed, and fearful of what other people think, and may have a feeling of helplessness.

The long-term effects of bullying on the victim could be PTSD, depression, long lasting mental health problems, difficulty in sleeping, concentration disorders, hyper-vigilance, and exaggerated anxiety reactions.

The list of health disorders can be quite long as a result of the extended stress, with developing children suffering from migraines, neurotic and psychosomatic disorders, gastric diseases, ulceration, and many other problems that can arise from being bullied.

What are the direct signs that your child may have become a victim of bullying?

1. They have noticeable injuries where the origin is hard to explain.
2. They provide improbable explanations concerning even the smallest injuries, i.e., I hit the locker, or I bumped into the door.
3. They come back home with their belongings damaged.
4. They often lose, or have damaged electronic devices.
5. They mention they don't have anyone close at school.
6. They stop showing interest in school.
7. They are afraid to go to school, or directly express fear of their friends.
8. They have started to get worse grades at school.
9. They isolate themselves, or explode in the middle of a conversation about school.
10. They often claim to be ill, and want to stay at home.
11. They often have head, back or stomach aches, and suffer from things like diarrhoea.

12. They start to exhibit eating disorders, either too small, or too big an appetite.
13. They refuse to change clothes in the presence of their peers.
14. They start to wet their bed at night.
15. They show signs of self-harm, (this is a big one), and show signs of poor mental health and self-esteem.
16. They show signs and symptoms of emotional disorders, and have intensive mood swings.
17. They neglect their appearance.
18. They become withdrawn, depressive, and behave childishly in relation with their peers.
19. They lose initiative, and don't build relations with others willingly.
20. They demonstrate tendencies to use alcohol and drugs.

Some typical cyber-bullying signs are:-
1. They stop using a phone, tablet, or laptop.
2. They show anger, anxiety, or sadness, during or after using webpages or phone apps.
3. They avoid discussing what they are doing online and what is going on there.
Naturally, in cases of cyber-bullying, typical symptoms characteristic with ordinary bullying may also occur.

So, how as a parent, do you intervene, and talk to your child?
1. A conversation should be the first step, but it should not be "is everything alright", but more of a deep and honest discussion.
2. Be honest with your child, and don't try and hide your emotions. If you want your child to open and frank, you need to behave in exactly the same way
3. You should find a quiet and safe place to talk, and sit so you are equal to your child.
4. You need to make time, switch off your phone, tablet, computer.

5. Follow your child during the conversation, they should feel that you are interested in what they are telling you, and not only in what you want to achieve.

6. When you feel that your child is open and relaxed, then ask them some open questions, such as, 'could you possibly tell me more about the incident', or 'I would like to understand what happened to you',

7. Remember, during the conversation they may cry, show fear, show pain, get angry or feel ashamed. It is very important for you not to deny their feelings, and don't trivialise them. Don't run away from these emotions.

8. It is very important you don't get angry, or cry, remember you are there to support your child.

There are some quite alarming figures when it comes to online activity and when children are online.

- According to research, 1 in 10 parents note that their child has suffered from offensive actions from a stranger, whereas, as many as 43% of the children researched, declared to have been offered a meeting from someone online, and 1 in 5 young internet users have actually met a person from the internet in real life.
- Only 1 in 5 parents think that their child has come across some pornographic materials or aggressive content, where in reality, 71% of children in the case of pornography.
- 51% of children, in the case of materials containing violence, suffers from such situations.
- Parents estimate that only about 1% of children suffer from cyber-bullying and cyber-violence, whereas, children state 47% of them experience some vulgar insults, 21% ridiculing or humiliating, 16% of children experience blackmailing, 14% of children experience publishing some discrediting contents.

Some more statistics which make very sad reading
- 57% children reported being bullied
- 28% children reported being cyber-bullied
- 7% reported carrying out forms of bullying
- 38% of children reported being physically bulled

- 86% reported being verbally bullied

If you have suffered trauma from bullying or cyber bullying in your life, and you want to regain control of your life, then there is help out there to release this trauma, and the best form of therapy for trauma from bullying is through hypnotherapy.

The Viking Buddha also offers 2 anti-bullying workshops for schools, the first being the Bullyproof program which is aimed at junior schools, and the 2nd being the High school bullying and cyber bullying workshop which is an intensive 1 day workshop.

Chapter 6
Trauma

What is trauma?

Many situations can be traumatic, and most of the time traumatic situations are unpredictable, and out of the person's control.

When somebody goes through a traumatic experience, they often undergo changes in their brain, and their bodies. This will most of the time, end up with the victim experiencing overwhelming feelings of anxiety and helplessness.

Trauma is an encounter resulting in severe psychological and physical stress. It can result from a single occurrence, or a series of events. No matter how long the trauma lasts, it can still cause harm, and effect a person psychologically, emotionally, physically and spiritually.

So a traumatic event is a singular incident such as a earthquake, fire, flood, burglary which causes emotional, spiritual, physical and psychological harm. After the traumatic event, the person may feel physically threatened, emotionally upset, and unsure how to respond.

They may also be in denial, and might behave as though the event didn't affect them.

Some common incidents which can cause trauma are:-
- Child abuse and neglect.
- Car crashes.
- Job loss.
- Fires.
- Sexual assault, rape or sex trafficking.
- Physical assault, murder or torture.
- Intimate partner violence.
- Suicide and poverty.

- Life threatening medical conditions.
- Earthquakes, floods, and other natural disasters
- Witnessing homicide or suicide.

Trauma can cause so much stress, and can be devastating for the person suffering with it. After a traumatic incident, there are numerous techniques that can be used to help the victim regain emotional equilibrium.

If symptoms of trauma persist, and affect a person's personal life, work life, school, sleep, etc, then it is time for that person to get help to deal with the trauma.

In children, trauma manifests in different ways, such as intense emotions, violent behaviour, difficulty sleeping, obsessive thinking about the experience. These are signs that a child may need help.

There are different types of trauma and below we will go through them:-

1. Community violence:- this is where it is predatory violence such as robbery, rape, stabbings, beatings, shootings, homicides, which people may experience as victims or witnesses.

2. Complex trauma:- This trauma is where the person is exposed to multiple or prolonged traumatic events over a period of time such as child abuse, domestic abuse, psychological maltreatment, neglect, physical and sexual abuse. Exposure to this kind of violence can affect a person deeply, resulting in emotional dysregulation, loss of safety and direction, deep anxiety, and the lack of ability to detect or respond to danger cues, which leads to subsequent or repeated trauma exposure.

3. Domestic violence:- this includes actual or threatened physical or sexual violence and also emotional abuse between adults.

4. Early childhood trauma:- this type of trauma generally refers to children aged 0-6, who have been subject to traumatic experiences such as childhood abuse, sexual abuse, witnessing domestic violence, natural disasters, sudden loss of parents, painful medical procedures.

5. Natural disasters:- this type of trauma generally comes from one off events such as tornadoes, hurricanes, earthquakes, fires, floods, explosions, but can also be caused by something like COVID19

6.   Refugee and war zone trauma:- this kind of trauma includes exposure to war, political violence, torture, and refugee trauma can be a result of living where there is bombing, looting, shooting, as well as being forced to leave their homes due to the above.

7.   School violence:-This includes teacher victimisation, bullying, cyber bullying, fights at school, and can cause problems many years after especially with things like bullying and cyber bullying.

PTSD

PTSD can have a significant effect on a person's life who is suffering with it, and their day to day lives and functioning.

The symptoms for PTSD normally develop in the first month after the traumatic event, but occasionally there might be a delay of sometimes months and even years before symptoms start appearing.

PTSD sufferers may go for long periods where their symptoms are not as noticeable, which can then be followed by periods where they are worse. For others there symptoms are always there, and can be made worse by triggers.

Symptoms of PTSD can vary from person to person, but on the next page are some of the symptoms which can be found in people who have PTSD

1.   Re-experiencing:- flashbacks, nightmares, distressing and repetitive sensations and images, physical sensations such as pain, Sweating, nausea and trembling. Others may have constant negative thoughts about the experience, which leads them to constantly question it, and prevent them from coming to terms with it.

2.   Emotional numbing and avoidance:- A person with PTSD may try in any way they can to avoid being reminded of the traumatic event, and this may mean avoiding certain places, people, that remind them of the trauma, and may avoid talking to anyone about their experience. Many people try to push the traumatic memories out of their mind, by distracting themselves

by doing hobbies or focusing on work. Emotional numbing is where the person tries not to feel anything at all, but this can lead to the person feeling withdrawn and isolated.

3. Hyperarousal:- Some people with PTSD may find it hard to relax, feel very anxious, and may be constantly looking for threats and may be easily startled. This unfortunately often leads to angry outbursts, insomnia, irritability, and difficulty concentrating.

Other problems with people who have PTSD may include:- depression, mental health problems, phobias, suicidal ideation, self-harming, substance abuse, destructive behaviour, headaches, chest pains, stomach problems, dizziness etc.

<u>PTSD in children</u>

Children with PTSD can have similar symptoms as adults, such as nightmares and insomnia. They can also have loss of interest in activities, headaches, stomach problems, difficult behaviour, avoiding things related to the traumatic event, and even re-enacting the event over and over in play.

<u>Complex PTSD</u>

Complex PTSD is when the person has repeatedly experienced traumatic events such as abuse, neglect or violence. This kind of PTSD is thought to be more severe if:-
- The parent or carer caused the trauma.
- The trauma was experienced over a long period of time
- the person was alone during the trauma
- there is still contact with the person who caused the trauma
- the events happened early in life

If this happened in childhood, it can affect the child's development, self-confidence and also create behavioural problems and other issues as they get older.

The symptoms of PTSD include
- difficulty in controlling emotions
- loss of attention and concentration
- feelings of shame and guilt

- headaches, dizziness, chest pains, stomach problems.
- Cutting themselves off from friends and family
- Relationship difficulties
- Self-harm, drug and alcohol abuse
- Suicidal thoughts

This is again just a short introduction to trauma, and is part of the bigger picture in this book about finding yourself, healing yourself, and finding your life purpose and the law of attraction and living your best life.

With regards to dealing with trauma and PTSD, talk therapies such as counselling, CBT, DBT, psychotherapy can help with coping skills etc, but if you really want to deal with the trauma and release it, then you need to be going right to the root of where the problem is stored, and that is your subconscious mind. The best way to deal with trauma and PTSD is hypnosis, EMDR, IEMT, etc, by using techniques such as trauma release, timeline therapy, narrative exposure therapy, and dealing with the problem so that it loses it hold on you, you can release it, and you are desensitised to it, so you can go forward in your life.

Chapter 7
Forgiveness

You have to forgive yourself, and let go of your past mistakes. You can't punish people for their mistakes. True justice is paying once for each mistake. True injustice is paying more than once.

Animals pay once for their mistakes, humans pay 1000's of times, as every time we remember, we judge ourselves, and feel guilty over and over again.

Many times in our lives we make mistakes, and we have to forgive ourselves for these mistakes. Most people have more resentment towards themselves than anyone else. There are two things that our minds unconsciously do when we feel guilty, one of them is to try to repay or make right our mistake, often excessively if we feel that there is nothing we can do to make something right. The second option we choose (unconsciously), is to punish ourselves.

Take a moment to reflect on your actions towards yourself, or others in the past that you may regret. Are there any mistakes you made that you continue to beat yourself up for?

How are you punishing yourself for it?

Are you directly or indirectly punishing others for it?

Your guilt is not going to undo what has happened. Even more importantly, holding onto this pain is causing further pain in your life.

You are missing out on a great deal in your life, if you don't know what it feels like to forgive. People often struggle to get past painful memories in their lives, and they dwell on the past, creating a downward spiral of pain and disappointment.

Forgiveness is a gift that you give yourself, and the people you love. The problem is people say they have forgiven, but still bring up the past, which just shows that they haven't truly forgiven. If you truly forgive somebody, then the past should remain in the past, and shouldn't be brought up again.

What forgiveness actually does, is that it gives both you, and the person you feel has wronged you, the freedom to move on. When you carry the burden of not forgiving somebody, you carry it with you for your whole life, which diminishes your ability to experience true happiness.

Forgiveness allows you to lift the burden and to see life from a different perspective.

The true art of forgiveness is when you can look inside yourself, and see no hatred, and feel no negativity, or any strings attached to past bitter experiences.

When people are angry, it is very hard for them to understand that forgiveness works in two ways. On one hand, it lets someone get away with actions that are unacceptable, and this is the side that most people see, but on the other hand, it lets you get away without all the bitterness.

There is ultimately a difference between forgiving someone, and condoning their actions.

Forgiveness also opens up a path to empathy, and empathy allows you to become more of a complete person who can peacefully co-exist with others whose opinions differ from your own.

Try this… the next time someone hurts you, don't wait for them to apologise, break the ice, and give them a call, to get the relationship back on track. It isn't about you forgetting what they did to hurt you, it is about you releasing yourself from it, and moving forward, because it really does not matter who apologises first, as long as there is forgiveness. If the other person cannot apologise, then they are always going to be in a weaker position.

The fact is that you imprison your heart when you are not able to forgive. You are actually imprisoning yourself when you cannot forgive, not the person you cannot forgive.

You are the one suffering from the anger, negativity, hate, lack of trust, and all the other things, and they may, or may not be feeling anything at all. It doesn't matter, the only thing that matters, is that you forgive the other person, and free yourself from the hot piece of coal you are holding onto, and let go and forgive.

We are all made up of energy. That is all we are, energy, and if we cannot forgive, we give off this negative energy, and other people around will avoid us, and this negative energy.

So many people hold onto grudges, and learn nothing from them. Instead of holding onto grudges and hate, tell them what they did wrong, regardless of if they apologise, and move on, let it go.

The art of forgiving others and moving on shows your strength of character, and what you do then is move on, and learn from the experience.

The next time something bad happens that gets you annoyed and frustrated, try not to let the emotions control you.

Don't react to negative emotions, just take a step back, and look at the situation calmly, forgive others, and look for a positive solution.

To forgive someone, is to put aside all the thoughts of anger, and revenge, and when you can do that, it is called absolute forgiveness.

"The truth is, unless you let go, unless you forgive yourself, unless you forgive the situation, unless you realise that the situation is over, you cannot move forward" Steve Maraboli

"True forgiveness is when you can say, thank you for the experience" Oprah Winfrey

"Forgiveness has nothing to do with absolving a criminal of his crime, it has everything to do with relieving oneself of the burden of being a victim, letting go of the pain, and transforming oneself from victim to survivor" C R Strahan

Today is the day for you to find the freedom in forgiveness.

Chapter 8
Gratitude

Be thankful for what you have! I will say that again.. Be thankful for what you have...

For a start, you never know what someone else is going through, so be kind to people... always be kind. There is an old saying, don't judge someone unless you have walked a mile in their shoes, and have experienced their life, and what they are going through.

Be thankful for what you have and stop comparing yourself to others, you are awesome yourself!

One of the most important things for you to have, is gratitude, to be grateful for what you have. No matter how educated you are, talented you are, rich or cool you think you are, how you treat people ultimately tells all. Integrity is everything, and you find in life sometimes those who have little, have the most to give.

- If you have food in your fridge, clothes on your back, a roof over your head, and a place to sleep... you are richer than 75% of the world.
- If you have money in the bank, and some spare change, you are among the top 8% of the world's wealthy.
- If you woke up this morning with more health than illness, you are more blessed than the 1 million people who will NOT survive this week.
- If you have never experienced the danger of battle, the agony of imprisonment or torture, or the pangs of starvation, you are luckier than the 300 million people alive and suffering.
- If you can read, you are more fortunate than 3 billion people in the world who cannot read.

Never forget on any day, you can step out of your front door, and your whole life can change forever... most people don't realise that they are just one decision away from a completely different life.

As the old saying goes "don't judge anyone, unless you have walked a mile in their shoes, and you have experienced their pain, and their problems, and what has happened to them in their lives.

Unfortunately, there are many people living in poverty around the world, and many people living on the street, many through no fault of their own, and it is normal for people to walk past them, ridicule them, and look down on them... but you do not know their story, you don't know their circumstances, and what trauma and heartache they have been through, and as I mentioned above, we are all just one decision, or one bit of bad luck away from being where they are.

So next time you walk past someone on the street, be grateful for what you have, and be grateful that you are not in their situation, and show gratitude, empathy, and show some love.

AD Williams once said... *"Imagine what 7 billion humans could accomplish if we loved and respected one another.. Just imagine... imagine if there was no greed, imagine if there was no comparison, if everyone was running their own race, but cheering for all others at the same time"*

Maybe we will never see that in our lifetime, but what we can do, is start with ourselves, start with YOURSELF... choose to lift others up, choose to set the example, the example of kindness and integrity, the example of compassion and understanding, because integrity is everything, it really is.

Who you are is far more important than what you have, and it always will be.

"Who you are is measured by how you make others feel, so be kind to each other, and in a world where you can be anything... BE KIND.... choose to be the change you wish to see in the world, you set the example. Be kind because you never know how much that person is suffering inside, you never know the difference your words can make, the difference your presence can make, the difference YOU can make to one human life. Always do what is right. You see kindness spreads like a virus, when you do good to another, that person does better to those who they come into

contact with, you really can make a difference in the world today and every other day"

Anne Frank said *"in the long run, the sharpest weapon of all is a kind and gentle spirit"* Nobody has ever made themselves great by showing how small another person is. BE KIND.... and always build others up to the best of your ability, treat everyone with the same level of kindness that you would like for yourself. Because karma makes no mistakes, and it is watching. We go on to talk about the law of attraction, and what you give out you get back, so be kind to everyone you meet.

One of the practical demonstrations I perform in my workshops, and motivational speeches, is about privilege and gratitude, and it goes like this... I hand out a blank A4 paper, and get people to crumple the paper into a ball and say *"you all represent the country's population and everyone in the country has a chance to become wealthy and move into the upper class. And the way to move into the upper class, is all you are going to do is take your crumpled piece of paper, and throw it into the bin from your seats".*

The moral of this exercise is, the closer people were to the bin, the better their odds were of getting the paper into the bin, and that is what privilege looks like. What is generally noticed is that the ones who complained about fairness were the ones in the back seats, whereas, by contrast those in the front seats were less likely to even be aware of the privilege they were essentially born into.

All they could see was the 5 feet between themselves and the goal. What the people who are more privileged need to do is be aware of their privilege, and to use this privilege and do their best to achieve great things, but also advocate for the ones who are not as privileged, the ones in the back seats.

Another interesting exercise about privilege, is where people stand up in a line, and questions are asked such as, how they were brought up, how they are financially, single parents, and about differences in people's lives and how this affected them, and the privileged people step forward, and the others stay where they are. At the end of the exercise, you see an interesting story of why some people end up starting their journeys in a much more advantageous position.

This was also done in a prison setting in the USA, where the prisoners were all asked to stand in a circle, and step forward if any of the questions they were asked applied to them. The type of questions included if they lived in poverty, were they brought up by a single parent, any abuse, trauma, not being able to afford to eat, and many other negative things were asked that might have happened to them.

While you can't excuse the crimes, you get to see a picture of how some of these inmates were thrown into a different life, and in some cases didn't stand a chance, and it is interesting to ask the question of the more privileged amongst us, what would we have done in their shoes? What would we be like if we had to walk a mile in their shoes, and have the upbringing and life they had growing up?

It really is about being grateful for what you do have in your life, because remember this, your terrible job is the dream of the unemployed... your house is the dream of the homeless... your smile is the dream of the depressed... your health is the dream of those who are ill... don't let the difficult times make you forget your blessings.

Chapter 9
Family & what is important

Here's a question for you to start this chapter off with...When you are in your final days of your life, what will you want? Will you hug that college degree on the walnut frame? Will you be asked to be carried out to the garage so you can sit in your car? Will you find comfort in re-reading your financial statements?

Of course not! What will matter most then will be people... so, if relationships will matter most then... shouldn't they matter most now?

Robin Williams once said *"as we go through the phases of our lives, we find ourselves trying to remember the good times, and trying to forget about the bad times, we find ourselves thinking about the future and start to worry, thinking, what am I going do?, where am I going to be in 10 years? But I say to you, hey don't worry so much, because in the end none of us have very long on this earth, life is fleeting, so make your life spectacular"*

A professor walked into his class, and started talking to his students *"We all have this one life to live, a fleeting shadow amongst all existence in this vast universe. We have the ability to accomplish anything, truly anything, if we use our time wisely"*

He then proceeded to take out a jar and some golf balls, some pebbles, some sand and two bottles of beer. He put the golf balls in the jar and said *"is the jar full?"* to which the students replied yes... he then put pebbles into the jar and again asked *"is it full now?"* to which the students again replied yes... he then proceeded to pour sand into the jar and again asked *"how about now, is the jar full now?*

He then got one of the beers, and poured one into the jar... and he then sad something that is so important in life.

*"Now I want you to recognise that this jar represents your life... the golf balls are the most important things...your family, friends, your health, your passions... the pebbles are the other

important things your car, your job, your home... the sand is everything else, just the small stuff.... now if you put the sand in the jar first, you won't have room for the pebbles or the golf balls, the same is true in life...

if you spend all your energy and your time on the small stuff, you won't have time for all the really important things in your life that matter to you.... pay attention to the things that are CRITICAL to your happiness. Take care of your golf balls first, the really important things, set your priorities, because everything else is just sand" what does the beer represent, well it just goes to show that no matter how full your life may be, there's always room for a couple of beers with a friend.

Life really is fleeting, and flies by so fast, one minute you are young, with your whole life ahead of you, and the next, you are in the later stages of life. Making the most of your time with family, your loved ones is so important, because one day they won't be here for you to spend time with them, and nobody knows what is around the corner. So spend time with your loved ones now!

I would like to share a poem which was written by an old man in a nursing home written for the nurses. It is quite poignant and really does make you think. You see as you get older, you may get slower, and unable to do the things physically like you used to, but inside you feel like that young person you once were. The poem goes like this...it's called the CRANKY OLD MAN

"What do you see nurses, what do you see? ...What are you thinking, when you're looking at me?

A cranky old man, not very wise... Uncertain of habit, and faraway eyes.

Who dribbles his food, and makes no reply...When you say in a loud voice, I do wish you'd try.

Who seems not to notice, the things that you do...And forever is losing, a sock or a shoe.

Who resisting or not, let's you do as you will... With bathing and feeding, the long days to fill.

Is that what you're thinking, is that what you see?.... Then open your eyes nurse, you're not looking at me

I'll tell you who i am, as I sit here so still...As i do at your bidding, as I eat at your will.

I'm a small child of ten, with a father and mother... Brothers and sisters, who love one another.

A young boy of 16, with wings on his feet... Dreaming that soon now, a lover he'll meet.

A groom soon at 20, my heart gives a leap... Remembering the vows, that i promise to keep.

At 25 now, i have young of my own... Who need me to guide, and a secure happy home.

A man of 30, my young grown so fast... Bound to each other, with ties that should last.

At 40, my young ones have grown and are gone... But my woman is beside me, to see i don't mourn.

At 50 once more, babies play around my knee...Again, we know children, my loved one and me.

Dark days are upon me, my wife is now dead... I look at the future, I shudder with dread.

For my young are all rearing, young of their own...And i think of the years, and the love that I've known.

I'm now an old man, and nature is cruel... It's jest to make old age, look like a fool.

The body it crumbles, grace and vigour depart... There is now a stone, where i once had a heart.

But inside this old carcass, a young man still dwells... And now and again, my battered heart swells.

I remember the jobs, I remember the pain... And I'm loving and living, life over again.

I think of the years, all too few, gone too fast... And accept the stark fact, that nothing can last.

So, open your eyes people, open and see...

Not a cranky old man, look closer, see ME....

Time really is precious, make sure that you spend it with the right people, and if you want to feel rich, just count all the gifts you have that money can't buy.

A wife said to her husband "I love you", he says "I love you too" her reply was " prove it, scream it to the world", her husband whispers in her ear, " I love you", his wife says, "why did you whisper it" and the husband replies "because you are my world"... Remember who and what is important in your life.

Time really is short and does pass by so quickly, so spend it with loved ones. If your parents are getting on in life, spend quality time with them as much as you can, as when they are gone, you can't turn the clock back.

We all lose family and friends along the way, and we don't know when our time is up on this earth. I lost my father in 2010, after a short illness with pancreatic cancer, and at the same time my twin daughters were born at 29 weeks, and one was born with a condition called TOF's, and at one point, I had one of the twins in one hospital, the one with TOFs in another hospital having 4 hour major surgery at one day old, and my father in another hospital dying of cancer.

I had to make the hard decision that I couldn't spend the last few days with my father before he died. I got to see him right at the end, before he died, as my daughter needed me more. So cherish the moments with your parents, your loved ones and children, because they don't stay children for very long

Life really is fleeting, and really is short, and in the end money, cars, houses, materialistic things don't matter. What really does matter is the people around us, our parents, children, and family and friends. I am the luckiest man in the world, and that is because I was lucky to have the best parents in the world, I have 5 amazing children whom I am so proud of each and every one of them, and although I haven't found my person yet, sometimes it takes longer to find that special person for some of us

Remember if your life revolves around work, and you don't see family that much, just remember this...

You are totally replaceable at work. You are not replaceable at home... Home is your real life.

Your parents don't need your tears when they die, They want your hugs, love, laughter, and care while they are still alive… and I am sure there are many people out there who put their parents off, and say we will come and see you soon, and then one day, the time has passed by, something happens, and you wish you could turn the clock back, just to spend one more day with them, and to spend some time with your loved ones…. Don't wait for that to happen, make those memories now, and spend that all important quality time with your family now…

Tomorrow is not promised to anyone, so, dance until your feet ache, laugh until your side hurts, say I love you to those you love, for tomorrow may never come…

Chapter 10
Cancer

Over the next chapter, I hope to show you why Cancer is not actually disease, but it is your body's last ditch attempts to wake YOU up to the abuse your body has been put through.

- We all know that smoking is bad for your body, and your health, yet there are many who continue to smoke, not knowing what changes are happening inside their body as their body tries to fight to keep the person's body in homeostasis.
- We all know that alcohol is bad for your body, and your health. (Yes it is a drug and poisonous to your body.. Doh..), Yet many people keep drinking not realising how hard their body is working to balance their body.
- We all know that meat is bad for us, especially red meat, as the body takes such a long time to digest meat, which is sometimes left putrifying in our colon and gut for years.
- We all know that processed foods are full of chemicals, and preservatives just to keep them from going off. There have been tests on certain fast food delights that when left out, did not start to go off or get mouldy for many months, yet many people stuff their body with processed foods, and think that their body will continue to be fine even though we abuse it so much.

FACT

Cancer and other debilitating disorders are not actual diseases, but instead they are desperate attempts by the body to stay alive for as long as circumstances permit!

It would perhaps astound you to learn that a person who is affected with the main causes of cancer (which constitute the real illness), would most likely die quickly unless he grew cancer cells.

Cancer will only occur after the body's main defence or healing mechanisms have already failed.

In extreme circumstances, exposure to large amounts of carcinogens can bring about a collapse of the body's defences within several weeks or months, and allow for rapid and aggressive growth of a cancer tumour, but generally it takes many years, and even decades for the so called 'malignant tumours 'to form and become noticeable diagnostically.

Here is a novel thought.... what if... cancer is actually on our side and not against us.

Unless we change our perception of what cancer really is, it will most likely resist treatment.

So, what if cancer is indeed part of the body's complex survival responses, and not actually a disease.

Cancer can be the greatest opportunity to help restore balance to all aspects of your life, but it can also be the harbinger of severe trauma and suffering. You are always in control of your body!

The human body must have a certain amount of life sustaining energy. You may either use this inherent energy in a nourishing and self-sustaining way, or in a destructive way.

If you choose negligence or self-abuse over loving attention and self-respect, your body will very likely end up having to fight for its own life.

So, in a nutshell, the main issue is not whether you have cancer...but how you perceive it.

Cancer, is one of the many ways that your body tries to change the way you see and treat yourself.

FACT:- damaged or faulty genes do NOT kill anyone
Cancer does NOT kill a person afflicted with it.

Would you like to know what really kills a cancer patient? What kills a cancer patient is NOT the tumour, but the numerous reasons behind cell mutation and tumour growth. These root causes should be the focus of every cancer treatment.

Have any of you suffered from trauma, guilt, shame, resentment and Stress? Constant conflicts, resentment, guilt, shame, stress, can easily paralyze the body's most basic functions, and easily lead to the cancerous growth.

Many cancer patients are burdened by some sort of poor self-image, past emotional conflict, trauma, unresolved conflict or issue, worry, that still lingers in their Subconscious mind and cellular memories. Yes, cellular memories, we will get that later in the book.

FACT:- The physical disease cannot occur, unless there is a strong undercurrent of emotional uneasiness and deep-seated frustration.

Many cancer patients may suffer from a lack of self-respect or worthiness, and often have unfinished business in their life. Cancer can help them come to terms with such conflict and even heal together. The way that you deal with weeds, is that you pull out the weeds, along with their ROOTS.

FACT:- It is a medical fact that every person has cancer cells in their body, at ALL times in their life. Let me say that to you again.

EVERY person has CANCER cells in their body at ALL TIMES in their life. The thing is though, these cancer cells remain undetected through standard tests until they have multiplied to several billion. Yes several billion! We have around 36 trillion cells in our body.

Curing cancer has nothing to do with getting rid of a group of detectable cancer cells.

Here is another fact for you:-

Treatments like chemotherapy and radiotherapy are capable of poisoning or burning many cancer cells, but they also destroy healthy cells in the bone marrow, gastro-intestinal tract, liver, kidneys, heart, lungs, which leads to permanent irreparable damage of entire organs and systems of the body.

Let me ask you a question. What do you think causes the falling out of hair, and sickness, and not being able to be touched as it's too painful?. The cancer? No, the cancer isnt there to kill you. Why would an intelligent cell want to kill you, when in the end it kills itself? We will go through this more in detail later, but quite frankly your hair falls out, and it is too painful to be touched, because your body is inflamed due to the chemotherapy, and your immune system is so depleted due to the effects of these treatments.

The poisons of Chemotherapy drugs alone cause so much severe inflammation in every cell of the body, that even the hair follicles can no longer hold onto the strands of hair.

FACT:- Cancer can have no power or control over you unless you allow it to grow in response to the beliefs, perceptions, attitudes, thoughts and feelings you have, as well as the life choices that you make.

Another question. Would you be as afraid of cancer if you knew what caused it, or at least understood what its underlying purpose was? I don't think you would!

When you hold on to anger, resentment, fear, expose yourself to the sun, don't get enough sleep, eat junk food, the chemical additives, artificial sweeteners, can you start to see why your body eventually needs a way to make you see what you are doing to it, and that it is under pressure, and basically crying out for you to change, for a chance to heal itself.

Cancer is merely an indication that something is missing in our body, and in our life. Cancer shows that our physical, mental, and spiritual life as a whole is standing on shaky ground, and is fragile to say the least.

There is NO cancer that has not been survived by someone else, regardless of how advanced the cancer is. The problem is that when the cancer is diagnosed, the vast majority of cancers are NOT given a chance to disappear on their own. They are immediately targeted with a deadly arsenal of weapons such as Chemotherapy, radiation and also the surgical knife.

And unfortunately, this is when sleeping tumours that wouldn't have caused much harm to the body, may now be aroused into powerful defence reactions and become aggressive.

It makes absolutely no sense, that when you need to strengthen the body's most important healing system – the immune system – you would then subject yourself to radical treatments that weaken, and destroy the immune system.

FACT:- Did you know that chemotherapy is so poisonous, that leaking a few drops of the drug onto your hand, can severely burn it, and if it drops on a concrete floor they can burn holes in it, and the spilling of any chemotherapeutic drug in the hospital or anywhere En-route is classified as a major biohazard.

Just imagine the holes chemotherapy creates inside your blood vessels, lymphatic ducts, and organ tissues when you undergo infusion after infusion.

Yes, the drug kills cancer cells, but along with them, many of your healthy cells too.. Your ENTIRE body becomes inflamed.

"Chemotherapy and radiation can increase the risk of developing a second cancer by up to 100 times
Doctor Samuel S Epstein

"My studies have proven conclusively that cancer patients who refuse chemotherapy and radiation, actually live up to 4 times longer than treated cases
Doctor Jones, Professor, University of California

Suffering from a disease, means that there is something wrong with the human engine. Medical practitioners however are not trained to deal with root causes of chronic illness. Their training is dedicated to alleviating or shutting down the symptoms, that indicate the body is trying to deal with an underlying imbalanced situation. When you remove the symptoms, you actually suppress the mind and body's attempt to deal with the actual real underlying problem.

Temporary cancer shrinkage through Chemotherapy and radiation, has never been shown to cure cancer or extend life. In other words, you can live with an untreated tumour for just as long as you would with one that has been shrunken or eliminated by chemotherapy and radiotherapy.

The bottom line is that tumours almost never kill anyone unless they obstruct the bile duct or any other vital passages. And in primary cancers, the tumour is never health endangering or life threatening.

The fact is that chemotherapy has never been shown to have curative effects for cancer. In contrast, the body can still cure itself, which it does actually do in the first place by developing cancer. Cancer is really more of a healing response than it is a disease. The disease is the body's attempt to cure ITSELF from an existing imbalance.

FACT:- Chemotherapy can give the patient life threatening mouth sores, and it attacks the immune system by destroying literally billions of immune cells (white blood cells). It inflames every part of the body!

If you have cancer, you may well think that when you feel tired, it is unfortunately just part of the disease. This is rarely the case, and the feeling of being tired is more likely to be anaemia, which is a common side effect of chemotherapy drugs.

Did you know that Chemotherapy drugs can decrease your red blood cell levels? and this reduces the oxygen availability to the 30 trillion cells in your body.

By permanently damaging the body's immune system, chemotherapy has become a leading cause of treatment caused diseases, such as heart disease, liver disease, intestinal diseases, pain disorders and rapid ageing.

Let me say this again... cancer cells are not part of a malicious disease process. When the Doctor says the cancer has spread (metastasized) throughout the body, it is NOT the cancer cells purpose or goal to disrupt the body's vital functions, infect healthy cells, and kill you.

Self-destruction is not the theme of any cell unless it is old, worn out, and ready to be turned over. The simple fact is that cancer cells are like all other cells, and know that if the body dies, they will also die as well.

A cancerous tumour is neither the cause of progressive destruction, nor does it lead to the death of the body. The cancer cell does not have the ability to kill anything.

Do you know what actually leads to the demise of an organ or the entire body? The wasting away of healthy cell tissues, which results from deprivation of nutrients and life force.

The reduction of nutrient supplies to the cells of an organ is not caused by cancerous tissue, but the reduction of nutrition to the cells actually causes the cancer cells.

A cancer cell is a normal healthy cell, that has undergone genetic mutation to the point that it can live in anaerobic surroundings (an environment where oxygen is NOT available).

If you deprive cells of oxygen, which is their primary source of energy, some of the cells will die, but others will manage to alter their genetic software program, and mutate in a most ingenious way. The cells will be able to live without oxygen, and will adapt to derive some of their energy needs from such things as cellular metabolic waste products.

Here is another fact for you... the more infections that are suppressed through medical interventions and prevented, the less efficient the immune system becomes, as well as the liver, kidneys, lymphatic and digestive systems in keeping the body's cell tissues free from harmful deposits.

So, let me say this again... cancer is NOT a disease, it is the body's most desperate and final defence mechanism at its disposal.

It only takes control of the body when all other measures of self-preservation have failed.

The body is always trying to tell us if something is wrong, but it is only when it has tried repeatedly to warn us that we are causing irreparable damage, that it tries to tell us in more drastic ways, in a final attempt to try and get us to stop abusing our bodies.

If we are ever to truly heal cancer in a person's life, we must come to the understanding that the body while allowing some of its cells to grow abnormally is actually acting in its best interest.

FACT... Cancer is NOT an indication that the body is about to destroy itself.

You, as consciousness, soul and spirit, are the ONLY true source of energy and information that run your body. Your presence in the body, and what you do, eat, drink, feel and think, determine how well your genes are able to control and sustain your physical existence.

If you, the conscious presence, are no longer present in your body, the energy and information are withdrawn from every cell. We know this to be physical death, you are no longer present and your eyes are empty.

Cancer only strikes when there are parts of us that are not alive anymore, be it physically, emotionally and spiritually, and that unfortunately happens to many people long before they do actually do die the physical death.

Cancer can resurrect these congested, suppressed areas whether they are physical or non-physical in nature.

How do we start this resurrection? We can start to realise how deeply we have harboured intense negative emotions towards others, and ourselves, such as trauma, hurt, hate, anger etc, and at the same time notice that we have allowed certain foods, beverages, drugs such as painkillers, steroids and antibiotics to contaminate and congest our beautiful body.

Here is the wake up call!! Cancer is the wake up call...

How does it do this? It prompts us to take our life back when it is no longer meaningful.

Cancer only occurs when channels or ducts of circulation and elimination have been consistently blocked for a long time.

So, what is a cancer cell?

"It is a cell that has lost its ability to fulfil its pre-programmed responsibilities of ensuring balance or homeostasis in the body. Instead of fulfilling its natural duty, such a cell has turned itself over to a new line of occupation that you could describe as a 'sewer worker"

During every single day in your adult life, the body turns over about 330 billion cells. Out of these an estimated 1% become damaged in the process and turn cancerous. Thats 3.3 billion cells every single day that are damaged and turn cancerous.

Your immune system is programmed to detect these cells and destroy them through a highly sophisticated arsenal of weapons including T killer Cells.

The body's clean up force is so efficient and perfectly timed that the cancer cells stand no chance of surviving. It is essential for the body's own survival that these kind of cancer cells are created every day, as they make certain that the immune system remains stimulated to keep its self-purification and defence system up to date.

In reality, cancer is an extended immune system response, to help clear up an existing condition of congestion that suffocates a group of cells.

So, why would the immune system try to hinder the body's efforts to prevent waste products entering the bloodstream and killing the body?

The cancer cells are far too precious, and too useful for the body to eliminate them. Cancer cells do NOT randomly spread throughout the body, they lodge themselves in other places that are also congested, in other places that are oxygen deprived also.

So why would the immune system want to collaborate with cancer cells to make more larger tumours?

Because cancer is a survival mechanism NOT a disease.

"The body uses the cancer to keep deadly carcinogenic substances and metabolic waste matter away from the lymph and blood, and therefore from the heart, brain and other organs. Killing off cancer cells would in fact jeopardise its survival"

The body only attacks a cancerous tumour after the congestion that has led to the tumour growth in the first place has been broken up.

FACT... Normal cells turn cancerous when they do NOT get enough oxygen to do their metabolic work. Without cell metabolism, the body would turn cold and lifeless within minutes.

Without the use of oxygen, and to keep some sort of metabolism going, the cells have to mutate into anaerobic cells that are capable of utilising accumulated metabolic waste products, and delivering at least some of the required energy and heat in the body.

What happens when you eat meat?

Did you know that the most blood thickening agent is food protein, particularly if it is derived from an animal source. "When compared to a carnivorous animal like a lion or wolf, your stomach can only produce only 1/20th of the hydrochloric acid needed to digest such a concentrated meal"

The concentration of the hydrochloric acid in cats and wolves is at least 5 times higher than in human beings.

Most of the animal protein will therefore pass undigested into the small intestine where it will either putrefy (80%), or enter the bloodstream (20%).

With regular consumption of animal protein, including meat, fish, eggs, poultry, cheese, milk etc, more and more intrahepatic stones are formed in the bile ducts of the liver, and this reduces the liver's ability to breakdown these proteins.

Protein foods are the most acid forming and blood thickening foods, so when this protein ends up in the blood, circulating, it thickens the blood. To avoid a stroke or heart attack, the body will dump the proteins into the tissue fluid or connective tissue surrounding the cells. This process actually thins the blood (for now), and staves off the imminent threat of cardiovascular complications (for now).

The problem is this dumped protein begins to turn the intercellular fluid into a gel like substance, and nutrients that are trying to make their way to the cells get caught up in this thick soup, which increases the risk of cell death due to starvation.

To avoid cell death, the body then tries to remove the protein from the intercellular fluid, the body rebuilds the protein and converts it into 100% protein collagen fibre.

Over a certain amount of time, the build-up of waste in the cells deprives them of oxygen and nutrients and they start to suffocate in their own waste, and this dramatic damage of the cell environment leaves them with no choice but to mutate into abnormal cells.

Cell mutation does NOT occur because the genes of the cell decided to have a bad day, and decided to play malignant.

Genes do NOT switch themselves on or off without a reason.

FACT... genetic blueprints have NO control or power to do anything.

Genetic blueprints are merely there the help the cell reproduce itself. The problem is that the genetic blueprint becomes altered when the environment of the cell undergoes major changes.

With the reduction of cell oxygen concentration in the environment, the genes then generate a new blueprint, that enables them to survive without oxygen and use metabolic waste for energy.

ALL OF THESE ADAPTATIONS MAKE CANCER A SURVIVAL MECHANISM TO KEEP THE PERSON ALIVE, FOR AS LONG AS CIRCUMSTANCES PERMIT.

Certain fats such as trans fatty acids or trans fats also attach themselves to cell membranes, making it difficult for the cells to receive oxygen, glucose and water, and oxygen deprived, dehydrated cells become damaged and turn cancerous.

Do you know what kind of polyunsaturated fats lead to a high risk of skin cancer and other cancers? Vegetable oil, mayonnaise, salad dressings, and most brands of margarine.

Did you know that margarine is just one molecule away from being plastic?

"Cancer has only one prime cause. It is the replacement of normal oxygen respiration of the body's cells by an anaerobic cell respiration" Dr Warburg, winner of the Nobel Prize in Medicine 1931

"lack of oxygen clearly plays a major role in causing cells to become cancerous" Dr Harry Goldblatt, Journal of experimental medicine 1953

"oxygen plays a pivotal role in the proper functioning of the immune system, i.e., resistance to disease, bacteria and viruses. Dr Parris Kidd

"Cancer is a condition within the body, where the oxidation has become so depleted that the body cells have degenerated beyond physiological control" Dr Wendell Hendricks, Hendricks Research Foundation

"Starved of oxygen the body will become ill, and if this persists, it will die" Dr John Muntz, Nutritional Scientist

Protein-cancer connection

The protein-cancer connection came to light after large scale scientific studies including 'The China Study' which demonstrated a virtual absence of cancer among people who don't eat animal proteins.

Research has also shown that meat contains a number of carcinogenic compounds, including some that are formed during cooking or processing of meat including heterocyclic amines and nitrosamines. They also found that meat contains other potential carcinogens heme iron, nitrates, nitrites, hormones and salts.

All of these substances have been found to affect hormone metabolism, increase cell proliferation, damage DNA, and promote damage of cells, all of which can lead to cancer.

It has been estimated approximately 35% of cancer can be attributed to diet. According to the China study, and other cancer research over the past 60 years, cancer could actually become a rare illness if animal proteins were avoided altogether, along with cutting sugar, and processed food out of our diets, and also dealing with the psychological issues such as stress and trauma.

For a normal person, the immune system tackles and kills the cancer cells easily and quickly. So a cure is an end to a disease.

In cancer statistics, The American cancer society listed some of 'their' cancer cure rates as high as 45% to 55%, yet we read from other sources that the cure rate for conventional cancer treatment is less than 3%. So who is telling the truth? The answer is, the reason why ACS and other cancer societies claim such high rates is due to the fact that they use a '5 year survival' rate, i.e. ability to live for 5 years.

This basically means that if the cancer originates in the liver, and after 5 years you have no liver cancer, but you have lung cancer, you are still considered cured and your figure is added to the cure rate. Or you have cancer, and you survived for 5 years, but you died from the cancer treatment after 5 years and 1 day, you are still considered cured, according to their cure rate statistics.

Or you have been 'cured' of cancer by conventional treatment, and due to the destruction of your immune system caused by the toxic treatment, you fall sick by catching a simple cold or pneumonia, and you died, you are still considered 'cured' of cancer, and your name is added to the cure rate.

Of course the motive behind this is the profiteering of billions of dollars, that the medical and pharmaceutical companies get from existing and potential cancer patients.

The cancer statistics from alternative treatments, natural treatments, and holistic treatment protocols, shows that the cure rate is 90%. Natural cancer treatments have a 30 times higher cure rate than orthodox cancer treatments of radiotherapy, chemotherapy and surgery.

"The American people and most of the rest of the world's population have been brainwashed by television and every other media source to 'go to the doctor' at the least sign of any medical problem. But doctors don't know how to be well themselves, or how to get you well. If they did know, they wouldn't be dying of cancer, or other horrible diseases at the same – or greater – rate than the general population.

Dr Lorraine Day, MD

"My studies have concluded conclusively that untreated cancer victims usually live up to 4 times longer than treated individuals" Dr Hardin Jones, professor of medical physics and physiology, University of California, Berkeley.

If everything is left to medicine, the cancer will kill you, if not, the treatment will finish you off.

Cancer must not be treated like it is a bacterial invasion, and the patient will be healed when the bacteria has gone and the invasion has stopped. Cancer is a process of evolution, where the patient's own cells mutate and metastasize all over the body.

Cancer is a nutritional, toxic, environmental condition in the human body, and in most cases can be reversed successfully through the application of a sound nutritional approach, and common sense lifestyle changes.

"The cause of cancer is no longer a mystery, we know it occurs whenever a cell is denied 60% of its oxygen requirements. Cancer above all other diseases has countless secondary causes. But even for cancer there is one prime cause. The prime cause of cancer is the replacement of the respiration of oxygen in normal body cells by a fermentation of sugar. All normal body cells meet their energy needs by respiration of oxygen, whereas, cancer cells meet their energy needs in great part by fermentation. All normal body cells are thus obligate aerobes, and all cancer cells are partial anaerobes" Dr Otto Warburg, in the Prime causes and prevention of cancer.

"the basic cause of disease is no longer a mystery, the basic cause is the habits of improper diet, inadequate exercise, negative mental attitudes, and the lack of spiritual attunement, which combine to produce toxic conditions and malfunction of our bodies.

The elimination of the habits that cause illness is done through the positive approach of developing proper habits that cause health, combined with corrective techniques that remove the ill effects of our former incorrect ways" Stanley Burroughs

"Alternative medicine explores the stressors (environmental, chemical, biological, psychological and emotional) in a patient's life, that cause a weakening of a particular energy field, which in turn allows the manifestation of a disease condition in a weakened area. In order to maintain a state of health, all energy systems within the body need to exist in a state of balance or equilibrium. Imbalance leads to conditions of discomfort (dis-ease), which eventually spirals into ill health if not corrected. The Chinese and Indians (Ayurvedic Medicine) had worked all of this out thousands of years ago"

"Orthodox or allopathic medicine utilizes poisonous substances (drugs) in non-lethal dosages in order to suppress symptoms in an affected area. This approach neither addresses the cause of the disease condition, nor is it responsible for healing the patient. Rather the use of drugs often will temporarily mask the outer manifestations of the malady, while at the same

time drive the disease deeper into the body, only to reappear at a later date, as a more serious and chronic health threat. One of the many flaws of the orthodox approach is that it focuses on the disease condition itself, rather than the patient. The term Wholistic (or holistic) sprang up to distinguish those physicians whose gestalt considers all of the physical, emotional and spiritual energies interacting with the patient". Ken Adachi, in forbidden cures, Suppressed alternative therapies.

"17 out of 20 cancer victims shouldn't have cancer, they have been murdered by the callous indifference of the people with power" Dr Vernon Coleman, F.R.S.M, Sunday Independent, November 1987

"And we have made ourselves living cesspools, and driven doctors to invent names for our diseases" Plato

"If I contracted cancer, I would never go to a standard cancer treatment centre, cancer victims who live far from such centre have a chance" Professor Georges Mathe, French Cancer Specialist

"chemotherapy and radiation can increase the risk of developing a second cancer by up to 100 times"
Dr Samuel Epstein, Congressional Record, Sept 9, 1987

« *Chemotherapy and radiation do not make the body well. They destroy, they do not heal. The hope of the doctor is that the cancer will be destroyed without destroying the entire patient. These therapies do kill cancer cells, but they kill a lot of good cells too, including the cells of the immune system, the very cell that one needs to get well. If a cancer patient survives the treatment with enough immune system left intact, the patient may appear to get well at least temporarily, but they will have sustained major damage to their body and their immune system. How much better is it to nourish the immune system directly by the use of natural therapies to assist it in getting you well instead of destroying it by the use of the conventional therapies. Then the immune system itself can kill the cancer cells without any side effects and heal your body at the same time"* Lorraine Day MD, Woman who cured herself of breast cancer naturally

Mangosteen Fruit

The mangosteen fruit contains Xanthones – biologically active plant compounds, which have many properties including antioxidants, and potent COX2 inhibition to reduce inflammation and pain.

Xanthones in mangosteen have the ability to eradicate and destroy cancer cells.

Not only does it induce apoptosis (programmed cell death) of the cancer, but it effectively destroys cancer cells resistant to modern chemotherapy treatments.

One In Vitro study showed garcinone E, a xanthone, to be more effective than 5 commoly used chemotherapy agents. As a COX2 inhibitor, mangosteen blocks production of Prostaglandin E2 impeding promotion and progression of cancer when DNA damage occurs, and it also attacks tumour cells directly.

Guyabano / Soursop

This is the natural cancer killer. It fights cancer cells, lowers blood pressure and increases the immune system. The Guyabano tree, its fruit, leaves and bark, is a natural cancer cell killer. A scientific research study in 1976 shows that one chemical is 10,000 times more potent than the chemotherapy drug Adriamycin.

Extracts from the tree were shown to effectively target and kill malignant cells in 12 types of cancer, including colon, breast, prostate, lung and pancreatic cancer.

What's more, unlike chemotherapy, laboratory tests show that the compound extracted from the Guyabano tree selectively hunts down and kills only cancer cells. It does not harm healthy cells.

A study at Purdue University found that leaves from the Guyabano tree killed cancer cells among 6 human cell lines, and were especially effective against prostate, pancreatic and lung cancers.

The Guyabano tree consists of many chemicals, but what makes the Guyabano tree special is that the tree contains a natural compound named 'acetogenins'. Research has found that this compound can slow the growth of tumour cells, and it is toxic to tumour cells without harming healthy cells. The tree produces the acetogenins in the leaves, stem and bark, and you can drink the extracts of the tree and this will help you fight against cancer.

Oberlies et al (1995) researched the capability of acetogenins to block, or inhibit the cell growth of tumour cells, and they tested this on several cell types.

Results showed that the more acetogenins were added with the cancerous cells, the more the cell growth was blocked, and in addition to this, the non-cancerous healthy cells were not affected by the acetogenins and the cell growth was not blocked.

Sodium Bicarbonate

An oncologist in Rome called Dr Tullio Simoncini discovered that Bicarbonate Soda destroys cancer cells.

Sodium Bicarbonate is safe, inexpensive and unstoppably effective when it comes to cancer tissues. It is an irresistible chemical, and it is a cyanide to cancer cells, as it hits the cancer cells with a shock wave of alkalinity, which allows more oxygen into the cancer cells that they can't tolerate. Cancer cells cannot survive in the presence of high levels of oxygen.

Sodium Bicarbonate is an instant killer of tumours.

The Bicarbonate maple syrup (molasses as an alternative to maple syrup) cancer treatment focuses on delivering natural chemotherapy in a way that it effectively kills cancer cells, but significantly reduces the brutal side effects experienced with most standard chemotherapy treatments.

The bicarbonate maple syrup treatment is a very significant treatment which every cancer patient should be aware of, and it can be combined with other natural treatments.

This treatment works like a trojan horse. Cancer cells gobble up sugar so when you encourage the intake of sugar (maple syrup) it is like the trojan horse.

The treatment is a combination of pure 100% maple syrup and bicarb soda. When mixed and heated together, the maple syrup and bicarbonate soda bind together. The maple syrup targets the cancer cells (which consume 15 times more glucose than normal cells), and the baking soda which is dragged into the cancer cell by the maple syrup, being very alkaline forces a rapid shift in ph killing the cell. The actual formula is to mix 1 part baking soda, with 3 parts (pure 100%) maple syrup in a small saucepan. Heat for 5 minutes, take 1 tsp several times a day.

The apple cider vinegar ¼ teaspoon and ¼ teaspoon bicarb soda, taken 2 or more times a day is another treatment, as is lemon and bicarb soda. Honey may be able to be substituted for the maple syrup if you are unable to get the maple syrup.

Breuss cancer treatment

Rudolf Breuss a healing practitioner from Austria said cancer can only live on the protein of solid food, therefore, if you drink nothing but vegetable juice and teas for 42 days the cancerous tumour dies off while the body continues to do well. Do not drink more that half a litre per day. The cocktail is made up of beets, carrots, celery roots, black radishes and potato.

The recipe is 300 grams red beets – 100 grams carrots – 100 grams celery root – 30 grams black radish – and potato. Mix all the vegetables in a juicer and strain to get rid of any sediment.

The actual Breuss instructions are:-

1. First thing in the morning – ½ cup of cold kidney tea
2. 30-60 minutes later, 2 cups of warm herb tea made from st johns wort, peppermint and lemon balm
3. After 30-60 minutes take some vegetable juice and salivate well before swallowing
4. 15-30 minutes later, another sip of vegetable juice. You should take some juice throughout the day.
5. In between drink warm or cold sage tea without sugar, as much as you like, and at noon and in the evening, half a cup of kidney tea.

No other food should be consumed during the treatment.

Anti-cancer fruit and vegetables

1. Garlic:- garlic can help stop cancer-causing substances from forming in your body, speed DNA repair, and kill cancer cells.

2. Broccoli:- it contains a compound called sulforaphane, and this helps boost the protective enzymes in the body and flush out cancer causing chemicals. It also targets cancer stem cells. Eat it raw or steamed

3. Tomatoes:- tomatoes owe their red colour to a phytochemical which is called lycopene. This is an antioxidant and it has been shown to stop the growth of certain cancer cells, such as breast, lung and endometrial. Watermelon, pink grapefruit and red bell peppers also have lycopene.

4. Berries are among the best source of antioxidants. They also contain ellagic acid which has cancer preventing properties which can destroy cancer causing substances and slow the growth of tumours

5. Carrots contain carotenoids, beto-carotene and alpha carotene. Beta carotene is believed to slow cancer cell growth, and protect cells from damage caused by toxins

6. Apples contain Polyphenols, which can prevent inflammation, cardiovascular disease and infections. Some research also shows polyphenols may modulate certain processes that lead to cancer development, and furthermore, another study in 2018 shows that apple phloretin inhibits growth of breast cancer cells without affecting healthy cells. The polyphenol inhibits a protein called glucose transporter 2, which plays role in advanced cancer cell growth.

7. Walnuts contain a substance called pedunculagin, which the body metabolises into urolithins, and these bind to estrogen receptors and may play a role in preventing and fighting breast cancer

8. Dark chocolate contains polyphenols, flavanoids and antioxidants and may have preventative effect on cancer. Research in 2022 also showed that people who ate more chocolate had a 12% lower risk of death from cancer.

9. Grapes contain resveratrol which has shown promise as a tool for fighting cancer.

Miracle Mineral Supplement (MMS)

The 3 things that all cancers have in common are
1. The body is overwhelmed with toxins and waster matter
2. The immune system is weak and depleted
3. There is a large presence of pathogens inside and around the cancer cells, which may include bacteria, viruses, parasites, fungi and yeast.

There is one substance, sodium chlorite which may have the most immediate and balanced effects on all of the diseases causing factors listed above.

The product MMS (miracle mineral supplement) is a stabilised oxygen solution of 28% sodium chlorite in distilled water.

The magic happens when you add a small amount of lemon or lime juice, or citric acid to the MMS as chlorine dioxide is formed. Once the chlorine dioxide is ingested, it oxidizes harmful substances such as parasites, viruses, bacteria, yeast, fungi etc within a matter of hours, and at the same time it boosts the immune system 10 fold.

MMS doesn't cure anything, it allows the body to heal itself.

There are many other natural remedies, and therapies for cancer treatment which include IV Vitamin C, water fasting, The Budwig Diet, The Keto Diet, intermittent fasting, Raw Vegan diet, green juice diet, Epigenetic Diet, Coley's toxins, Bob Beck Protocol, Black Cumin Seed oil, Alkaline water, Pao Pereira, Oxalic acid, Fenbendazole – turmeric, CBD oil, Bee venom, and may other treatments. I don't cover them in this book, but I do go a little more into them in the 3 day 'Awakening' Workshop, and also in private and group sessions.

The other really important factor in healing from cancer is the emotional and psychological part. It has been proven that trauma, stress, anger, and all other negative emotions cause cancer and your body to break down with dis-ease.

It is so important to rid yourself of deep rooted trauma and stress, and even if you don't think you have any trauma, or negative emotions in your body, you most likely do, and clearing these emotions is the most important thing for you to do for you to heal from cancer.

The best way to ger rid of negative emotions and release trauma, is through hypnosis.

I have the greatest respect for the nurses, health care assistants, and other support staff, surgeons in hospitals around the world, and many doctors also, who do an incredible job caring for people, but I think medical professionals need to start looking at how they are treating their patients, and is it to benefit the pharmaceutical companies, or do they truly want to help their patients.

When my father was diagnosed with pancreatic cancer, I went to see the oncologist, the 'medical professional', who, when I said I was an alterative medicine therapist, called me a 'witch doctor', to which we then had an interesting conversation as to how toxic the chemotherapy drug was, and what would happen if we put this on her hand, let alone inside her body.

Eastern medicine, alternative medicine, 'voodoo medicine' as this oncologist saw it, has been around for many thousands of years, and I think it has done pretty well to help people over that time.

Western medicine, conventional 'orthodox' medicine, has been around a couple of hundred years, and it not about dealing with the cause, but with the symptoms, and 'popping pills'. Yet cancer was virtually unheard of for thousands of years, as was diabetes and many other diseases, but in the time of modern medicine, cancer is on the increase, diabetes is at its highest level ever at the moment, and many other diseases are increasing including asthma, and this is because they are treating the symptoms, and not actually what is really behind the body being in 'dis – ease'.

I have two people come up to me recently saying they were palliative and nothing they could do, and it astounds me that a medical professional would give this negative information to someone. There are two words which many doctors should look up in a dictionary. 'Placebo', which is when something positive is said to someone, and 'nocebo', which is where a doctor says, 'sorry, you are going to die'. This is crazy!

Because that person, looks at this 'trained' professional, and actually listens to those words, and believes them because, hey he is a doctor. So what happens? That person then starts to deteriorate, because the doctor said they are going to die, so they are going to die... What utter rubbish!

I remember working as a support worker in the community, and being called out to this lady who had kidney disease, and she refused to have dialysis and the doctors then very wisely, advised her that if she didn't have dialysis she had around 6 months (with their crystal ball of course).

I went to talk to this lady, and basically told her to forget what the doctors, nurses etc said, and asked this lady what she loved to do. She said 'I love going on cruises', to which I said, 'go and enjoy yourself, go on cruises, enjoy, and have fun'. Do you know how long this lady lived? It was about 18 months later, I heard she had passed away.

The nocebo effect, especially coming from a doctor, will have that exact affect and that person will do exactly as that person said they would and die. The placebo affect has the opposite effect on the brain and the psyche, and gives that person hope.

Another gripe of mine with regards to oncologists and cancer wards, is that, as you have seen in this chapter, meat is a carcinogenic, and feeds the cancer. Sugar, cakes, sweets, and any other things containing sugar etc, feed the cancer, it is like giving the cancer cells a wonderful meal. The cancer cells love glucose remember, and as you will see in the next chapter, with someone who has cancer, we need to get the body into an alkaline state, and not in an acidic state. It is beyond belief that medical professionals are still saying to people with cancer to eat meat and sugar, and feeding the cancer.

Later in the book, we are going to be looking at epigenetics, neuroplasticity and quantum embodiment, and how YOU can turn your lives round.

The thing is, the doctor doesn't cure you! The therapist doesn't cure you! They can be a catalyst to help you get better, but you cure yourself, you heal yourself.

Even with hypnosis, the hypnotherapist is a catalyst, the give you suggestions, but it is YOU who heals yourself, and it is YOU who cures yourself. And as epigenetics, and neuroplasticity will show you later in the book, it is NEVER too late to change your life and heal yourself.

www.thevikingbuddha.com

Chapter 11
Alkaline Nutrition

So, what is the Alkaline diet?

In order for your body to function optimally and healthy, you need to maintain a PH level of 7.35-7.45, which is the perfect range for oxygen to be carried around your body.

The modern Western diet, filled with processed food, fast food, and a lot of meat and dairy, not to mention alcohol, sugar and caffeine, is acid forming, which means your body has to work really hard to digest the food, using minerals which would be better off used elsewhere.

A PH above 8 is alkaline, below 7 is acid, and 7 is neutral.

When we have eaten, and it has been digested, and we get the energy from it in the form of calories, our digestive system acts like a slow burning fire, where it burns the food to get the energy, and when that fire burns out, it is left with ash, and this ash can either be acid or alkaline depending on the food that you have eaten.

If you eat a lot of sugar, fried food, refined food, processed food, this leaves you with an acidic ash, which over time, will lead to chronic inflammation, a weakened immune system, and leaving you prone to disease.

Within our body we have organs that are masters at neutralising acid ash, but over time it can get overwhelmed, when it is working constantly, without any respite, and then it starts to overload and fail.

With alkaline nutrition, we are not trying to alter the blood pH, we are taking a load off the system so that it doesn't have to work as hard, to make it more efficient again.

This is why we need to eat more alkaline forming foods such as fruit and vegetables, grains, seeds nuts etc, and avoid the acid forming foods such as meat, processed foods, sugar, fried foods, dairy products, fatty foods and caffeine

The letters Ph stand for power of hydrogen. The hydrogen scale ranges from 1 (acid) through to 7 which is neutral to 14 (alkaline)

For our body to perform at an optimum level, the important fluids in our bodies need to be slightly alkaline, 7.365 to 7.45

The most important level which has to stay constant is your blood level, which needs to maintain 7.365 to 7.45. But here lies the problem. Your pH levels aren't on your standard 1:1 scale. It is logarithmic to the tune of 10. So, 6 is 10 times more acidic than 7.... 5 is 100 times more acidic that 7.... 4 is 1000 times more acidic than 7.... And 3 is 10,000 times more acidic than 7. The soda you drink comes in at 10,000 times more acidic than what where you want your body to be.

The problem is when your pH is lets say at a 5, and 100 times more acidic, it has to come from somewhere to bring it to where it needs to be at 7.365 to 7.45.

After the food has been broken down in the stomach, and small intestines, it is in this part of the digestion where the acidic or alkaline ash has a direct impact on your pH. If the ash is alkaline, then the body doesn't have a great deal to do, we have enough acids to bring it to the level we need.

But if the ash is acidic, then your body has to release alkaline buffers to neutralise it, and this is usually taken from the calcium in your bones.

With the poor food and lifestyle choices that many people have, our body is having to work extremely hard to neutralise the acid, which eventually leads to low level chronic inflammation, stealing calcium and minerals from your bones to make up for the bad lifestyle choices you make.

When your body is in a constant state of acidosis, this is very destructive to you body and can lead to the following conditions below

- Hypertension, stroke, heart disease
- Kidney stones
- Type 2 diabetes
- Cancer
- Infertility

- Bone problems and osteoporosis
- Dis-ease

Whereas, an alkaline diet, and a balanced pH leads to
- Healthier colon
- Lower cholesterol
- Weight loss
- Stable blood sugar
- Healthy immune system
- Increased energy
- Reversal of metabolic syndrome
- And goodbye to headaches, acid reflux and slow digestion.

Chapter 12

Talk Therapies / Coping Strategies

In this Chapter, we delve into what kind of therapies are out there to help with the issues and problems people may have in their lives, such as Mental Health, Stress, fears phobias, trauma, PTSD, addictions etc.

I qualified as a Remedial Hypnotist / Clinical Hypnotherapist in 2005, and then over the years to become a more rounded therapist, I have added more qualifications and training to my repertoire, such as Stress Management, Mental Health, Alcohol addiction, NLP, EMDR, CBT, DBT, SFBT, REBT, Existential Therapy, Psychodynamic Psychotherapy, Gestalt Therapy, Narrative Exposure Therapy, MBSR, Metacognitive Therapy, Transformational Life Coaching, and also training in Bullying and Narcissistic and Domestic Abuse.

I did this for 2 reasons primarily.
1. Not everyone wants to be hypnotised and I will go more into hypnosis in the next chapter on hypnosis.
2. Different modalities and styles of Therapy can help different people, and can get the best results, and my aim has always been to get to the point where I can help as many people as I can, and get the best possible outcome for my clients.

With The Viking Buddha, we are setting up Workshops, Groups, individual sessions for people to deal with their issues and problems, and also in 2025 we are looking at our first retreats / Dark Retreats in the UK, Jamaica, Nepal and the USA.

Over the next few pages I want to go into a brief overview of some of the Cognitive / talk therapies which are available out there which can help people with their problems and issues.

CBT

CBT stands for Cognitive Behavioural Therapy. We have the ability to control our thoughts, emotions and our behaviours. CBT is an integrated therapy which combines both cognitive and behavioural approaches. The basic goals of CBT are to change the way a person perceives things to more positive and appropriate ways, and also to change the behaviours of the person to create more positive outcomes.

DBT

DBT stands for Dialectical Behaviour Therapy, is also a type of Cognitive Behavioural Psychotherapy, which can be used for treatment for different kinds of mental health disorders, and for people who experience extreme emotions. It is a type of talk therapy, which can help people cope with painful emotions, through acceptance and change, and helps people to achieve the changes required to be able to better cope with these emotions. It focuses on the thinking and behaviour of the person, stress management, problem solving approaches, and the person's own self-awareness.

It can be used for various issues, problems and disorders including mood disorders, self-harm, substance abuse, stress related conditions, Borderline Personality Disorders and trauma. So, in a nutshell, DBT helps the person focus on changing unhelpful ways of thinking and behaving, whilst at the same time accepting who they are. Dialectical basically means trying to balance opposite positions, and looking at how they go together, for example, acceptance, and accepting who you are, and change – making the positive changes in your life

REBT

Rational Emotive Behaviour Therapy is based on the idea that events alone don't cause the person to feel anxious, angry, or depressed. It is actually more about the beliefs regarding the events which contribute to the unhealthy feelings and behaviours.

So, it isn't about the actual event that causes the stress to the person, it is more about how the person actually views that event, and to what extent they find it upsetting or negative.

REBT is a solution orientated therapy, which is focused on resolving emotional, behavioural, and cognitive problems with people, in order to produce positive outcomes.

REBT works by getting the person to examine their own ideas, beliefs, thoughts and assumptions, and test them, and through REBT, and this process, this hopefully gives them more logical and helpful beliefs to move forward with.

SFBT

Solution Focused Brief Therapy is a form of psychotherapy, but it is slightly different than other forms of therapies.

This type of therapy is solution focused, whereas other forms of therapy are problem focused, and spend more time talking about the problem.

SFBT is more about understanding the person's strengths, and what strengths and resources the person has already, and getting them to talk about the future they would like. So basically SFBT tries to focus on the future that they want, rather than endlessly talking about the problem. So you can see how this type of therapy can work well with other forms of therapy such as CBT, DBT, as it can offer an all-round form of therapy, dealing with the problem and solution leading to the preferred better future.

Gestalt Therapy

This is more of an experiential and relational way of working with people, and more holistic in its approach. It is focused on the person's awareness of how they are living their life, and how they manage their relationships. It also focuses on self-awareness, and the here and now, as being self-aware is the key to personal growth and the development of their true potential.

The problem with some people is that their self-awareness can be blocked by negative thought patterns and behaviours, and that can lead to people feeling unhappy and dissatisfied in their lives. It is very much focused on the person starting to become aware of their own self, their own emotions and feelings, and being in the present moment.

There is a wonderful exercise in Gestalt therapy called the empty chair technique, where a person may perhaps have quite deep rooted emotional problems, and this exercise helps the clients get engaged in different roles during the session, and can talk about emotional difficulties, and it's purpose is to get the patient to think about their emotions and attitudes.

The empty chair is 'occupied 'by the imagined person, part of the client, a feeling (depression / sadness) that can be spoken to by the person.

The empty chair technique can bring the person to experience different aspects of their own conflicts, and can be used for unfinished situations from the past, in which the person is not available in the present

Existential therapy

This is another form of psychotherapy, which is based on the model of human nature and experience. It focuses on human experience including the meaning of life, responsibility, freedom and death. This type of psychotherapy allows the person to explore their own individual experiences, while stressing the person's individual freedom to facilitate a higher meaning and well-being in their lives.

There are many other different types of cognitive / talk therapies available, which are used by counsellors, therapists, Psychotherapists, and I could write a book on its own about the many different types of therapies which are available, and their different approaches, but ultimately, they can be used as part of a toolbox and integrated in a way to find the best solution and best treatment for people, giving them the best ways to cope and move forward with their lives.

Chapter 13
The Power of Hypnosis

This is, and always will be the best form of therapy for me. Yes I am slightly biased towards the power of hypnosis, but having treat many people over the years using hypnosis, I have found this by far the most effective therapy available.

As discussed in the last chapter, Cognitive / Talk Therapies are excellent in helping people to look at themselves, their behaviours, finding coping skills and strategies, accepting and finding solutions for their problems, and helping them move forward with their lives with these new found coping skills. They are also good for reframing of behaviours.

But ultimately, they are techniques dealing with the conscious mind, and not actually dealing with the trauma, phobias, fears, but helping the person to cope with their feelings associated with the trauma etc.

To be able to actually deal with the real issues such as trauma, PTSD, phobias, addictions, you have to go much deeper, and these issues are stored in the subconscious mind.

With hypnosis, we are able to access the subconscious mind directly, and it can have amazing results.

My Background and training in Hypnosis goes back to initially training in hypnotherapy back in 2004, then I wanted to take that further and train in hypnosis from some of the best celebrity and renowned hypnotists, and that has led me to where I am today.

The problem that many people have with hypnosis, and hypnotherapy, is that there is still a stigma there caused by stage hypnotists, and this confusion as to what hypnosis actually is. Many people come to me and ask, "can you control what I do", "can you make me do things I don't want to do", and there is this belief that as an hypnotist I can make someone bark like a dog, or eat a raw onion.

So to put that record straight, hypnotists can't make you do anything. On stage an hypnotist will find the best subjects who are more susceptible to going into an hypnotic trance, and once that trance state has been accessed, and they are happy being hypnotized, their boundaries are stretched a little, and they do some fun things on stage.

If you felt uncomfortable or in danger, you would wake up quickly, and come out of hypnosis and here is why…

Hypnosis is a natural state. We all go in and out of hypnosis on a regular basis. Let's say for instance you are driving your car, and then you get to your destination and think 'how the hell did I get here?', that is a light trance state. The same thing is going into a supermarket, where you go into buy 4 or 5 items and come out with much more, and wondering why you have bought those items. You go in and out of light trances so to speak many times in a day.

Hypnosis has been described as deep relaxation, or an heightened awareness, and we could go into the different brain waves etc, but for the purpose of this book, I don't want to go that deeply into things such as that.

Hypnosis is basically where we bypass the analytical conscious mind (where talk therapies work with), and we access the subconscious mind, which is where all your trauma, fears, phobias, habits, and any other issues are stored.

Once we have accessed that part, the hypnotist will then give suggestions to release trauma, deal with fears and phobias and other problems, and this happens because the subconscious is happy to accept these suggestions and implement these changes.

So, there is no mind control, all the hypnotist is dong during therapy, is taking that natural trance like state what you enter regularly, and deepening that state through hypnosis, allowing you to focus on their voice and allowing their suggestions to make changes whilst in that state to deal with your problems, rather than just give coping strategies.

In essence, we are going direct to the root of the problem, and releasing the trauma, helping the person to lose weight through suggestions to the Subconscious mind, or helping a person to quit smoking by making the cigarettes taste vile, or by giving other suggestions direct to the subconscious mind for many different problems and issues.

Hypnosis can help with so many different problems that it would take so long to list them all, but your spider phobia you have had for years can be dealt with in most cases in one session.

Pain can be managed through hypnosis, habits and addictions can be treated through hypnosis.

The list of things that can be helped with hypnosis is endless, as what you are doing is going into the most powerful part of your body, your mind, and you are accessing your Subconscious mind to deal with YOUR problems.

The hypnotist doesn't heal you, they are the catalyst, they give you suggestions which your Subconscious mind then accepts and makes those changes.

Trauma can be dealt with and released in just a few sessions through trauma release, timeline therapy, regression techniques.

"the best way of explaining hypnosis is we have a CPU and hard drive, and in between we have a firewall. With cognitive therapies such as counselling, CBT, DBT, they rely on cognitive speech, they are after the hard drive, I am not interested in that, not the family photos, your downloads, and dodgy videos you may have picked up, I am interested in the CPU, the driver, where the fight flight freeze response hangs out" Karl Smith

I think the quote above from one of the best hypnotists around at the moment, describes hypnosis in a great way. In hypnosis, we are accessing the CPU, the driver, and we are going straight to where the problem is kept.

We are dealing directly with that problem, head on, and making life altering changes, which allows the person to get their life back, to release the issues holding them back from having that full and happy life. This is where hypnosis, NLP and to a degree EMDR etc differs from cognitive therapies, as instead of just giving coping skills to people, where they still have the underlying issues stored in the deepest parts of their mind, but are given coping skills to basically mask the problem, at best, hypnosis deals with those problems head on and can literally transform lives, as I have seen many, many times.

Another question I regularly get is 'can everyone be hypnotised?' and the simple answer to that is… Yes! Because we all go into light trances, and hypnosis is really just focus, relaxation and imagination.

If a person wants to be hypnotized, they will be hypnotized. If a person wants to deal with their issues, stop smoking, lose weight and get rid of phobias and trauma with the help of an hypnotherapist, those issues will be dealt with through hypnosis. It is a very powerful technique and can literally change your life.

If you want to book sessions either face to face, or online via zoom etc, you can do so by going to the
Website:- www.thevikingbuddha.com
email thevikingbuddha@yahoo.com
or telephone +44 0330 043 3203

Chapter 14
Cold Water Therapy

In this chapter I just wanted to do a very brief overview of what is becoming a very popular pastime for some people, which is the popular pastime of wild swimming and cold water therapy, and to show the wonderful health benefits that this type of therapy can offer.

Cold water therapy is where the person basically immerses their body into cold water or ice (officially 21 degrees Celsius or lower) which is said to awaken the body's own healing processes which can aid in many different conditions and ailments including:-

- Mental Health Issues
- Auto Immune Issues
- Obesity
- Type 2 diabetes
- Inflammation
- Chronic pain
- Stress & Burnout
- Circulatory problems.

There are many more health benefits to cold water therapy, and it is becoming widely used by many people

Cold water therapy can be done in a number of ways from taking cold showers and baths at home, to wild swimming in the sea, rivers and lakes. Wild swimming has other benefits too because being out in nature means you are exposed to Phytoncides.

Phytoncides are compounds emitted by trees and plants, which enable them to fight off bacteria, fungi and viruses, and for us, these compounds are excellent for our immune system.

There are many other benefits to cold water therapy including:-

- Resilience to stress
- Improved Vagal Tone

- Improved Immune system
- Improves Insulin sensitivity for type 2 diabetics
- Improves thyroid function
- Improves circulation
- Can help with pain relief
- Can help with depression and anxiety
- Helps with sleep and insomnia

This was just a very brief outline of the benefits of cold water therapy, and I would highly recommend you do further research into this type of therapy which is incredibly beneficial for your health and wellbeing.

Chapter 15
Complementary Therapies & Natural Remedies

This Chapter is about introducing complementary and holistic therapies into your lives, and the benefits they can have on your body and mind.

I have been a massage therapist and clinical reflexologist since 2005, and I am very much Eastern Medicine orientated, and studied quite intensively on Natural remedies, holistic approaches, and the healing plants and the natural sources of healing that surround us. There are many different types of massage available, and I would like to focus on the particular ones I personally provide for clients.

Swedish Massage

The Swedish Massage is the traditional type of massage that is available. It is a whole body therapeutic massage, that works with the muscles and soft tissues to help restore health. It has many benefits including:- alleviating muscle pain, better sleep, improving posture, increasing blood circulation, it improves flexibility and range of movement in muscles and joints, it helps to remove toxins, increases overall energy, and improves the immune system.

Indian Head Massage

The Indian Head Massage has been used for over 4,000 years in Indian Culture, and is an incredibly beneficial massage which focuses on the upper back, neck, head and face, and it's benefits include aiding in the relief of headaches and migraines, it promotes hair growth, stimulates lymphatic drainage, relieve insomnia and fatigue, it relieves symptoms of anxiety and depression, renews energy levels, and boosts memory capabilities, amongst many other benefits, and is a very relaxing de-stressing massage.

Lomi Lomi Massage

The Lomi Lomi Massage is a deep healing massage from Hawaii and ancient Polynesians. It is a more spiritual massage, with different techniques which may feel like waves of the ocean, which help to restore balance and harmony. It is a more gentle massage and looks at things like energy flow. There are many benefits including relieving tension in muscles, improving muscle nutrition, stimulating the immune and lymphatic system, easing headaches, stress and tension, detoxifies the body, clarifies the mind, and many other benefits.

Clinical Reflexology

Being a clinical reflexologist, and having had many clients over the years, this treatment is absolutely wonderful for bringing balance to the body and helping with so many conditions,

Reflexology dates back to over two thousand years to Egypt, India and China, and is a type of massage on the feet, hands and ears. It is based on the theory that your feet, hands and ears are connected to the organs of the body and body systems, and your body is mapped out on your feet and hands etc.

Vital energy or Qi flows through everyone, and when that person feels stressed, or there is a blockage, this causes an imbalance in the body that leads to dis-ease and illness. Reflexology can help clear blockages and keep the energy flowing through the body keeping it balanced and dis-ease free.

There are many benefits to reflexology including, reducing stress and anxiety, improvement of wellbeing, reduced pain, improved immune system, it can help fight cancer, it can help with hormonal imbalances, boosts fertility, improves digestion, and can treat nerve problems.

The next part of this chapter is about natural remedies for different conditions. I have put some main conditions in this book, but there are many other conditions that can be healed with Natural remedies, plants and Eastern Medicine.

Western Medicine does have its part to play in helping people, and surgery etc is necessary in certain circumstances, but I am very much anti-Pharmaceutical drugs and western medicines, because they basically mask health conditions, whilst at the same time most of these drugs come with many side effects and are detrimental to health, not to mention the billions profit made by big Pharmaceutical companies.

It has been said there is a plant, fruit, vegetable, or other natural remedy on this earth for every single illness, ailment or disease. You just have to do your research, and find the things that can cure you.

Below are some of the main conditions and some natural cures and remedies. Whatever condition or health problem you have, do some research into these natural remedies, plants, aromatherapy oils, homeopathic remedies, and heal yourself naturally.

Acne

- Burdock root:- 300-500mg capsule form, 30 drops soft tincture, 1 cup of tea, 3 x daily.
- Vitex-chasteberry:- 160mg of standard extract or 40 drops tincture daily.
- Tea tree oil:- 5% solution tea tree oil in water, apply solution by dabbing it onto blemishes 2x daily.
- Avoid junk food and processed food, sugar, chocolate, alcohol and dairy products.
- Aromatherapy oils:- Lemongrass, lavender, chamomile and cedarwood.
- Saw Palmetto blocks excessive DHT of the sebaceous glands. 160mg extract or 30 drops of tincture 2x daily.
- Oregano oil destroys yeast overgrowth associated with acne formation. 500mg twice daily or use as liquid.
- A 3 day vegetable juice fast will sweep away toxic build up
- Acupressure points:- BL23, BL47, ST2, ST3 help clear acne.
- Reflexology:- kidneys, liver to detox blood, endocrine glands and also colon.
- Aloe vera gel controls acne. Echinacea also controls acne.

Allergies

- Vitamin C has a natural antihistamine effect and strengthens the immune system and is also an astringent. 1000mg 3-5x daily
- Stinging nettles:- effective for hay fever, 300-500mg daily.
- Quercetin:- 1000mg 3x daily. This is a natural antihistamine.
- Flaxseed oil:- reduces inflammatory responses associated with allergies. 1-2 tablespoons daily.
- Thymus extract:- this calms the immune response to allergies
- Probiotics:- These reduce the potential for allergies. Take a product containing at least 4 billion organisms.
- Acupressure:- LI4 relieves headaches and sneezing. BL10 for fatigue, swollen eyes and headaches. ST36 is a good all over toner and promotes balance within the body.
- Reflexology:- big toes and inside of heels helps abate allergic reactions
- Aromatherapy:- chamomile and eucalyptus for hay fever
- Aloe vera cream helps with allergies
- Echinacea:- this is a natural immunity enhancer, it also stabilises the histamine producing cells. A cup of echinacea a day boosts the immune system for the hay fever season.
- Garlic:- add garlic to diet 1-2 months before hay fever season as it contains B Group Vitamins that have immune boosting properties.
- Plantain juice or tincture:- anti-inflammatory and also acts to tone and dry the mucus membranes.
- elderflower:- Natural astringent which dries up mucus, it is an excellent preventative treatment for hay fever.

Alzheimers Disease

- ACETYL-L Carnitine:- improves brain cell communication and memory, 1000mg 3x daily.
- DHA:- take fish oil supplements that contain daily dosage of 1000mg. DHA improves brain function.

- Gingko Biloba:- improves circulation to the brain and improves memory. 120mg 2-3x daily.
- Club moss:- this increase acetylchlorine levels in the brain and improves memory.
- Vitamin B12:- 800-1000mg daily.
- Vitamin E:- slows progression of alzheimers. 2000IU daily of a complex with added locotrinol
- Ashwagandha:- brain tonic in ayurvedic medicine, it reduces stress hormones. 100-300mg daily
- Cordyceps sinensis:- used in Chinese medicine for poor memory. 2-4 capsules daily
- NADH:- improves mental function. 10mg daily
- Vitamin B1:- Has been shown to improve mental function in people with alzheimers disease. 3gms daily.
- Acupressure:- ST36, tones entire body. GV24.5 strengthens both memory and concentration. PER6 for anxiety and nervous. LU1 ease depression and encourage deep slow breathing.
- Lymphatic massage:- detoxifies the body, while improving circulation, including circulation to the brain.
- Reflexology:- lymph system to detox tissues and cells. Heart to encourage blood flow to the brain. Lungs to oxygenate the blood.
- Aromatherapy:- juniper helps break down toxins

Anaemia
- Iron:- 50-100mg iron 1-2x daily
- B12:- 1000-2000mg daily
- Folic acid:- 800-1200mg daily
- Brewers yeast:- good source of iron, folic acid and B12 1tbsp daily
- Spirulina:- improves production of red cells. 2000mg daily
- Nettle leaves:- 300mg 2-3x daily
- Homeopathic:- ferrum phosphoricum, 5 pellets of 3x or 6x potency daily. Improves iron utilization in cells.

- Dandelion root:- high iron content. Cleanses blood and detoxifies the liver. 3-5 gms daily
- Ashwagandha:- increases red blood cell count. 2000-3000mg daily
- Dong Quai:- builds red blood cells, 500mg 2x daily for 1 month
- Reflexology:- spleen to encourage the manufacture and recycling of haemoglobin. Liver to aid circulation, blood formation and detox.
- Aromatherapy:- eucalyptus, ginger, black pepper, and rosemary oil improve circulation.

Arthritis
- Glucosamine Sulfate:- 1500mg daily, and chondroitin sulfate 600-1200mg daily. Reduces joint pain and rebuild cartilage.
- Methylsufonylemethane:- 2000-8000mg daily. Anti inflammatory and contains sulfur which is an integral component of cartilage.
- Fish oil:- reduces joint inflammation and promotes joint lubrication, 1.8mg of DHA and 1.2mg of EPA.
- Eat plenty of cold water fish, salmon, mackerel, and also fibre vegetable and pineapple.
- Ginger:- relieves both inflammation and pain. 1-2 grams of dried powder in capsule 2-3x daily
- Cayenne cream:- symptomatic relief, apply 2-4x daily.
- Vit C and E, produce enzymes to reduce inflammation.
- Acupressure:- LI4 for hands, wrists, elbows, shoulders and neck. LI11 pain in elbow and shoulder. ST36 for entire body including joints
- Pineapple:- bromelain the enzyme in pineapple lessen the pain of swelling in soft tissues.

Asthma
- Practice the Buteyko method daily.
- Drink lemon juice diluted with cold water every morning as soon as you wake up. Between meals drink one teaspoon of undiluted lime juice.
- Aromatherapy oils:- clary sage, cypress, eucalyptus, frankincense, and marjoram
- Lobelia flowers:- make a potent respiratory stimulant which produces stronger deeper breathing
- Caffeine:- caffeine is very similar to theophylline, which is a bronchodilator drug that is taken to open the airways in the lungs. So during an asthma attack drinking a strong black coffee or a can of coca cola which contains caffeine can help relieve an asthma attack.

Back pain
- Methylsulfonylmethane:- alleviates muscle spasms and has a natural anti-inflammatory effect. 3000-8000gm daily in divided doses.
- Calcium and magnesium:- alleviates muscle spasms. 500mg calcium, 250mg magnesium 2x daily.
- Cayenne cream:- apply to area 2-4 x daily. Pain relief
- Arnica oil:- reduces pain and spasms. Rub oil on affected area 2x daily
- St John's wort oil:- reduces nerve pain. 2x daily.
- Acupressure:- BL25, BL31, BL40, lower back pain. BL20 middle back pain. GB20, GV14 upper back pain.
- Reflexology:- spine, hips, tailbone area.

Bladder infection (cystitis)
- Uva ursi:- destroys bacteria
- D-mannose:- prevents bacteria from attaching to urinary tract and bladder wall. 500mg 4x daily.
- Echinacea and goldenseal:- enhances immune system. 500mg capsule form, 4ml tincture, 4x daily

- Cranberry extract:- prevents bacteria from adhering to the bladder wall and also prevents urinary tract infections. 400-500mg 2x daily.
- Horsetail:- 500mg capsule, or 2ml tincture 4x daily.
- Vitamin C:- enhances immune system, inhibits growth of E-coli and makes urine more acidic so that bacteria cannot easily grow. 1000mg 4-5x daily
- Oregano oil:- anti-bacterial and antiviral. 500mg capsule, 4 x daily
- Reflexology:- bladder, kidneys, ureters.

Blood pressure (high)
- Hawthorn:- dilates artery walls and decreases blood pressure
- Coenzyme Q10:- 100mg 2-3x daily
- Garlic 600mg 2x daily
- Fish oil:- reduces blood pressure
- Passionflower:- relaxes nerves and stress. 250mg or 0.5ml 2-3x daily
- Reishi:- 500mg 3x daily
- Dandelion leaf:- natural diuretic to lower blood pressure 300mg or 2ml. 3x daily.
- Acupressure:-BL38, PC6, H3&7, CV17
- Reflexology:- thyroid, kidney, solar plexus, pituitary and adrenal glands.

Bronchitis
- N-acetylcysteine (NAC) reduces viscosity of phlegm. 300-500mg 2x daily
- Vitamin C:- Enhances immune system and anti allergy benefits. 500-1000mg 3x daily
- Echinacea and goldenseal:- enhances immune system and dries up mucus. 500mg or 2ml of combination 4x daily.
- Mullein:- promotes mucus discharge and anti-inflammatory effects on respiratory tract. 500mg or 2ml 4x daily.
- Astragalus:- strengthens lungs and increases bodies resistance to infection. 500-1000mg 3.5ml 2-3x daily.

- Colloidal silver:- anti-microbial. ½ to 1 tsp 3x daily for 5 days.,
- Garlic:- anti-microbial effects. 300-600mg 2x daily
- Licorice:- reduces coughing, enhances immune function, soothes respiratory tract. 500mg or 1ml tincture 4x daily.
- Acupressure:- relieve chest congestion – K27, CV22, LU1, LU7… Difficulty breathing – BL38

Burns
- Aloe vera:- soothing effect and stimulates skin healing. Apply gel to burned area 2x daily.
- L-Glutamine:- tissue healing and prevents secondary infection. 500-1000mg 3x daily.
- Calendula:- apply 2x daily
- Potato:- shred or mince an uncooked potato and place the pieces of potato on the burn, in 30 minutes or so, the redness of the burn disappears, sometimes the potato even prevents blistering
- Milk:- minor burns can be treat with milk, soak a cloth in milk and apply to burn
- Urine:- rub urine into the burn and redness will disappear and can prevent blistering.

Cardiovascular disease
- Garlic:- blood thinner and antioxidant. 300-500mg 2x daily.
- Co-enzymes Q10:- Used by heart cells to pump efficiently, and with regular rhythm.
- Fish oil:- daily dose of fish oil reduces inflammation in arteries, natural blood thinner, and lowers cholesterol.
- Hawthorn:- improves circulation to heart and reduces blood pressure. 500-900mg daily.
- Magnesium:- relaxes blood vessel walls, improves circulation, reduces blood pressure. 500mg daily.

- Gingko Biloba:- improves blood flow, antioxidant, blood thinning. 80-120mg 2x daily
- L-Carnitine:- lowers triglyceride levels and improves heart contraction. 500-2000mg daily.
- Cayenne extract:- reduces cholesterol levels and improves circulation. 500mg 2x daily.
- Acupressure:- if you have a heart attack while waiting, squeeze finger tips of little fingers, may reduce severity of attack

Common cold
- Echinacea:- improves immune system, 500mg or 2-4ml 4x daily
- Lomatium dissectum:- anti-viral. 500mg or 2-4ml 4x daily.
- Ginger:- helps with sore throat and chills. 500mg 4x daily.
- Astragalus:- excellent for preventing colds. 500-1000mg 0r 3ml tincture 3x daily
- Elderberry:- adults 10ml. children 5ml 3x daily
- Garlic:- for immune system, 300-500mg 3x daily
- Thymus extract:- optimises immune activity. 1-2 capsules 2x daily
- Acupressure :- LI4, K27, BL2, LI20, GB20, GV16. GV24.5
- Foot baths:- hot and cold foot baths alternate
- Reflexology:- toes, lungs, adrenals, lower spine, pituitary, lymph system, neck area.
- Aromatherapy:- immune system – lavender... relieve congestion and stimulate circulation – eucalyptus and peppermint... fights virus – tea tree
- Ice:- Icing big toes can abort a cold

Constipation
- Flaxseed oil:- lubricates colon for easier passage. 1-2tbsps daily
- Probiotic:- at least 4 billion organisms helps with digestion

- Dandelion root:- stimulates bile flow and improves circulation. 250-500mg or 2ml with each meal.
- Homeopathic:- nux vomica. 30c potency. 2x daily.
- Fenugreek:- improves bowel contractions. 250mg or 2ml 2x daily.
- Aloe vera juice:- improves bowel movements. Take ¼ cup 2x daily.
- Gentian root:- improves overall digestive function. 300mg or 10-20 drops. 5-15 minutes before meals
- Accupressure:- constipation and abdominal cramps – CV6... Intestinal contractions – LI4... strengthening colon LI11... strengthens digestive system – ST36
- Reflexology:- colon, liver, gallbladder, adrenal glands, solar plexus
- Cold water:- drinking one or two glasses of cold water on arising starts peristalsis.
- Dried figs:- for chronic constipation eat one or two dried figs on an empty stomach each morning.
- Acupressure:- the bony V in the web between thumb and index finger can help with constipation.
- Oatmeal:- to prevent constipation eat oatmeal eery morning.

Cough
- Liquorice:- reduces coughing, enhances immune system and soothes respiratory tract. 500mg or 1ml tincture 4x daily.
- Cherry bark:- reduces coughing, 500mg or 1ml tincture 4x daily
- Mullein:- helps with discharge of mucus and inflammation. 500mg or 2ml 4 x daily.
- Echinacea and goldenseal:- enhances immune system and dries up mucus, 500mg or 2ml 4x daily.
- Astragalus:- strengthens lungs and increases resistance to infection. 500-1000mg or 3.5ml tincture 2-3x daily.
- Garlic:- 300-600mg 2x daily
- Acupressure:- K27, CV22, LU1, LU7, BL38

- Fitzgerald technique :- gently press the middle of your tongue with a table spoon for 3-4 minutes. Repeat as needed in ½ hour intervals.

Diarrhoea
- Astragalus:- excellent treatment for chronic diarrhoea. 500-1000mg 2-3x daily.
- Activated charcoal:- binds toxins in the digestive tract. 2 tablets 3x daily.
- Probiotic with at least 4 billion organisms

Eczema
- Flaxseed oil:- reduces inflammation and dryness, ½ to 1 tbsp
- Burdock root:- cleansing effect on skin. 300mg capsules or 1ml tincture.
- Zinc and copper:- needed for skin healing. 30mg zinc, 3mg copper 2x daily
- Dandelion root:- assists liver in detox. 500mg 3x daily
- Quercetin:- anti-inflammatory. 1000mg 3x daily.
- Acupressure:- SP10 cleans heat from blood…. BL23 and BL47 relieve eczema,
- Reflexology:- liver, kidneys, intestines, endocrine glands, lymph, solar plexus.
- Cucumber:- wash and peel 1 cucumber, place slices of cucumber onto rash. The Ph of the cucumber is almost matched to the skin.

Fibromyalgia
- Magnesium:- relaxes nerves and muscles. 250mg 2-3x daily.
- Grape seed extract:- improves circulation and anti-inflammatory properties. 100mg 2-3x daily
- Passionflower:- relaxes the nerves. 300-500mg 3x daily.
- Valerian:- relaxes the nerves. 300-500mg 3x daily
- Probiotic:- will 4 billion organisms
- Flaxseed oil: pain relieving omega acids. 1-2 tbsp daily.

- Black cohosh:- balances hormones, and relieves spasms in muscles. 40mg 2x daily
- Arnica oil:- relieves muscle pain and tenderness
- Acupressure:- CV17 supports immune system and also eases depression and anxiety. LIV3 relaxes muscles and swollen nerves.
- Cordyceps sinensis:- supports adrenal gland function 800mg 2x daily.

Gout
- Celery seed extract:- anti-inflammatory and may reduce uric acid levels. 450mg 2-3x daily
- Nettle root:- encourages elimination of uric acid from kidneys. 250mg 3x daily
- Chlorella:- works on alkalising the body. 500mg 4 x daily
- Quercetin:-anti-inflammatory. 500-1000mg 3x daily.
- Devils claw:- 1500mg-2500mg 3x daily. Reduces uric acid in the blood

Headaches
- Magnesium:- alleviates migraine headaches. 200mg 2-3x daily
- Feverfew:- reduces severity, duration and frequency of migraines. 250-500mg daily
- Melatonin:- 0.3-0.5mg before bedtime
- Gingko Biloba:- improves circulation to the brain. 60mg 2-3x daily.
- Peppermint or menthol cream applied to temple are can help with tension headaches.
- White willow bark:- contains salicin, the ingredient which aspirin is derived. Effective pain relief. 60-120mg daily.
- Acupressure:- LI4 for front head pain… BL2 for headaches accompanied by tired painful eyes or sinus congestion… GC20 will ease headaches of any sort.

- White vinegar:- soak corner of handkerchief in white vinegar and hold to nose for 5 minutes, breathe deeply to inhale the smell.

Heart palpitations / Heart attack
- Place a pinch of powdered cayenne pepper on the middle of tongue as a traditional remedy to arrest an heart attack

Insect bites
- Lemon essential oil:- put on skin to repel insects and relieves pain of insect stings and bites
- Mix earth and water to make mud when outdoors and dab on bite to instantly relieve pain

Insomnia
- 5-hydroxytryptophan:- promotes serotonin production in the brain for relaxation. 100-200mg 1 hour before bed.
- Melatonin:- hormone promotes sleep. 0.3-0.5mg 1 hour before bed
- Passionflower:- relaxes the nervous system. 500mg or 1-2mls ½ hour before bed.
- Valerian:- effective for insomnia. 600mg or 1-2ml ½ hour before bed
- Chamomile tea:- relaxes the nervous system. Drink tea or 300mg capsule form.
- Aromatherapy:- lavender, neroli, chamomile, ylang ylang,

Memory loss problems
- Cayenne pepper:- sprinkle on food to help improve memory
- Bacopa:- improves memory and recall. 300mg daily
- Gingko biloba:- improves circulation to the brain and improves memory. 120mg 3x daily
- Club moss:- increases acetylcholine levels in the brain and improves memory
- Acetyl-L Carnitine:- improves brain cell communication and memory. 500mg 3x daily

- Panax ginseng:- improves memory and balances stress hormones. 100-250mg 2x daily
- Cordyceps sinensis:- good for memory. 2-4 capsules daily
- Reishi:- improves mental alertness. 800mg 2x daily
- Reflexology:- head, neck, liver

Menopause
- Black cohosh:- alleviates menopausal symptoms including hot flashes. 80mg 2x daily
- Natural progesterone cream:- alleviates symptoms and helps bone density
- Adrenal glandular extract:- supports the hormone producing adrenal glands. 1-2 capsules 2x daily
- American ginseng:- supports adrenal function, improves energy, relaxes nervous system and has cooling effect. 600-1200mg daily
- Rehmania:- reduces hot flashes, night sweats, heart palpitations and other menopausal symptoms.
- Reflexology:- uterus, ovaries, fallopian tubes, all glands, solar plexus, chest and lung.
- Hypnotherapy:- during trial studies through Viking Buddha, it has been found very effective for dealing with pain, joint pain, tiredness, and various other less talked about symptoms using different techniques under hypnosis
- Hydrotherapy:- a warm sitz bath will increase circulation in the pelvic area and will improve dryness and decreased libido.

PMS
- Vitex chasteberry:- 180-240mg daily for 4-6 months will improve symptoms
- Dong quai:- reduces cramps and breast tenderness. It also relaxes the smooth muscles of the uterus thereby relieving cramps. 300-500mg 2x daily. On the last 7 days of cycle.
- Crampbark:- alleviates menstrual cramps. 3ml or 500mg every 30-60 minutes for acute menstrual cramps.

- Acupressure:- CV6 AND CV4 reduce pain of menstrual cramps. Lower back pain work BL25, BL31, BL40
- Reflexology:- uterus, fallopian tubes, endocrine glands, lower spine

Substance abuse detox
- Milk thistle:- supports liver detox, and reduces elevated liver enzymes. 250mg 3x daily
- B Complex:- detox and mood and energy support. 50mg 2x daily
- Homeopathic:- nux vomica. Reduces withdrawal symptoms of irritability, nausea, constipation and fatigue. 30c potency. 2x daily
- Chromium:- reduces sugar and possibly alcohol cravings
- Reishi extract:- improves liver and immune system function, and helps with focus and concentration. 800mg 2x daily

These are just a few remedies for different conditions, and of course there are many more diseases and conditions and indeed remedies for the conditions available. If you need a consultation you can contact me at www.thevikingbuddha.com

In addition to natural remedies, many fruits and vegetables have healing properties and can help with many issues and although I am not showing them in this book, I would suggest more research on how to include these in a healthy diet to support your immune system and keep healthy.

Urine Therapy

The last subject in this chapter is a controversial one, but I would like to go through the 'science 'of this subject, and you can make your own minds up after more research.

Has your Mother or grandparent ever said to you after you have burnt yourself, or been stung by a jellyfish, to 'rub your own pee on it?'

I am sure many saw the episode on Friends TV series where this subject was brought up and was quite hilarious, but there is a lot of truth in this.

I once burnt myself a number of years ago and tried this by rubbing pee on it, and afterwards there was no redness or blistering. And on another occasion, someone asked me about a wart, and I said same thing, rub some pee on it every day, and sure enough a week or so later, it had gone black and fell off. So what about the 'science 'and 'facts 'about this controversial subject. Here we go...

Urine is often thought of as a waste product from the body, but this is actually incorrect. The lungs, skin, and digestive system all function to remove waste.

Only the kidneys can make urine. The main job of the kidneys is to maintain your bloods pH levels and filter waste products. Urine, is in effect, a sterile antiseptic fluid which contains a variety of elements that are actually necessary for life, and these include vitamins, minerals, proteins, enzymes, hormones, antibodies, and amino acids, and many other chemicals, which your body doesn't need at that time, and that is why it passed through and out of your body as urine.

Urine's other very significant substances include:- agglutinins, which block viruses... antineoplaston, which inhibits the development of cancer cells... Allontoin, which promotes wound healing, and DHEA which is used to treat female breast cancer, diabetes, anaemia... 3-methyglyoxal, which helps destroy cancer cells... prostaglandin, which is an hormone that relaxes bronchial muscles, and also widening blood vessels and lowering blood pressure... retine, which is a chemical isolated from urine, with anti-cancer effects... uric acid, which helps fight ageing... cortisone which is a well known healing agent... and urea, which is a major cause of urine's antimicrobial properties, to name but a few of the substances.

The main idea around urine therapy is that urine contains a range of compounds with therapeutic properties. Basically Urine therapy aims to recycle antibodies which each person produces and are excreted from the body through their urine, and when you re-enter this into the body, it is basically re-absorption of nutrients, hormones, enzymes, urea, etc, and it is kind of re-learning the body and helping it to fight any infections, viruses, bacterial infections etc, and it is said to have a bactericidal and virucidal effect, a diuretic effect, and also a detoxification effect, and is said to be able to help the body heal itself.

Now this again is quite a technical area, as we can go into why the re-absorption of urine supposedly works so well, but this is just an introduction on a controversial subject on whether it is actually waste, or the 'elixir of youth 'and cure for many illnesses. There are many studies and books out on this subject, but for now I will leave it up to you to maybe research and look into this fascinating therapy some more.

And this is where we end Part one of the book, and leave the pain behind, and move onto part 2 of the book and indeed the 3 day workshop which we run, called 'The Key to Your Life'

Part 2
The Key
To
Your Life

Chapter 16
Mindfulness

Now what better way to start the second part of this book and discovering the ways to find the Key to Your Life, than talking about Mindfulness, and being in the present moment.

So what is Mindfulness?
"Mindfulness is awareness that arises through paying attention, on purpose, in the present moment, non-judgementally" Jon Kabat-Zinn

"Mindfulness is the basic human ability to be fully present, aware of where we are and what we are doing, and not overly reactive or overwhelmed by what is going on around us" Mindful.org

"The practice of maintaining a nonjudgemental state of heightened or complete awareness of one's thoughts, emotions, or experiences on a moment-to moment basis" Merrian-webster-Dictionary

"Mindfulness is the act of being intensely aware of what you're sensing and feeling at every moment – without interpretation or judgement" Mayo Clinic

So mindfulness is about living in the present moment, and being aware of your feelings in every moment, and being able to live in that moment without judgement and feeling at ease and being one with the universe every moment. Living fully in the present.

Mindfulness is awareness, attention focus, being present and being vigilant. Whereas at the opposite is mindlessness, which is being distracted, showing lack of attention and lack on engagement. To be able to move forward in life and find the key to your life, you need to learn to live in the moment, live in the present, without judgement, and be aware of what is going on around you, but being able to not judge and stay positive and now allow things or people to affect you.

What you need to do is to start observing how you react to situations and others in a negative way, and learn how not to be a slave to our emotions and reactions, but instead learn how to step back and evaluate emotions before reacting negatively, and taking time to react in the right way and in the present moment.

"Your worst enemy cannot harm you as much as your unguarded thoughts" Buddha

Buddhism itself follows something called the 'eightfold path'
1. Right view:- we are all in a constant state of change and nothing is permanent, and anything that we do perceive as reality, is simply just a state that will pass. We have to acknowledge that suffering exists and that it is not permanent, it will begin, it will exist and it will end, and when we accept this, there lies a peaceful existence
2. Right intention:- we have to let go of all suffering, such as outcomes, control and harm to others, don't push it away, just notice it, observe it, and once you have identified it, let it go
3. Right speech:- be kind and honest. Let go of any angry, controlling, abusive language, be kind and listen to what others are saying
4. Right action:- do no harm to any other living being, and refrain from any negative physical action against others.

5. Right livelihood:- be honest, and avoid suffering to others and yourself, and don't partake in any immoral work or any dishonesty.
6. Right effort:- make sure all of your efforts are wholesome and right on a spiritual, physical and emotional level.
7. Right remembering:- be clear minded in your awareness, and do not cling to material gain and objects and ones emotions. Be aware of yourself and other people's emotions and live in the present moment.
8. Right belief:- keep your mindset, clear, constant and wholesome.

An ICM survey done in the UK with GPs found the following statistics.
- 72% of GPs think it would be helpful for their patients with mental health problems to learn mindfulness meditation skills
- 68% of GPs say that they would support a public information campaign to promote the potential health benefits of mindfulness meditation
- 64% of GPs think that it would be helpful to receive training in mindfulness skills themselves

Research shows that mindfulness training can benefit in many ways including:-
- Better attention and concentration, and clearer focus
- Less selfishness and greater ability to think about others more, and become more empathetic, compassionate and sensitive to others feelings.
- Greater insight:- when we become mindful, we observe what is happening around us, but we don't get caught up in things anymore, and we have greater clarity what is going on in our lives.
- More acceptance:- through mindfulness we start to realise that things are always changing, they never stay the same, thoughts, feelings and even events are always changing.
- We get greater enjoyment out of life because we become more aware of the wonderful experiences that are happening

around us in the here and now, and not putting our mental focus on the past and future.
- As we will discuss in future chapters, there is no such thing as the past or the future, it is an illusion, the only thing we have is now. The present
- Less negative thinking:- when we are mindful, we stop thinking about our thoughts, and realise that negative thoughts only harm us in the now and also are projected into our future, and we learn to life in the present and enjoy every moment.

Remember there are 3 main concepts when practising mindfulness. Awareness, being non-judgemental and living in the present moment.

There are many different exercises that can help with the practice of mindfulness, and they include Tai Chi, Qi Gong, Yoga, sound baths, Breathwork and meditation.

Meditation is a very important piece in the mindfulness puzzle, and meditation is just a simple way of focusing internally on the moment while being still, with no judgement, and being in the moment.

When looking at the benefits of meditation and how it can help with mindfulness practice it is easy to see why it is such an important piece in the puzzle.

It can help with:-
- Mental wellness, cognitive functioning and emotional control
- Reduction in anxiety, stress levels, depression and job burnout
- Improved awareness, heightened empathy
- Improved attention, better problem solving
- Slowing of brain ageing
- Strengthened immune function
- Improved sleep
- Reduction in chronic pain
- Lowered risk of cardiovascular disease

And many more benefits…

Breathwork is another fantastic part of mindfulness, as this allows you to focus on your breathing, and with different breathwork techniques this can improve our focus, how you breathe and breathing correctly and it can help with various health conditions too. The other benefits to doing breathwork regularly are:-
- Releases toxins from your body
- Increases energy and boosts the immune system and Strengthens your lungs
- Increases self-awareness
- Eliminates chronic pain
- Helps with digestion process
- It can release trauma and fear
- You can explore altered states of consciousness

Shinrin Yoku
This section is taking mindfulness a little step further!
I have always had a love of nature, and being outside, and the mountains, and have climbed many a hill and mountain, including going to Everest Base Camp in 2017.
Nature has many healing health benefits, and there is no better place to start than Shinrin Yoku otherwise known as Forest Bathing.
Shinrin Yoku is a very special mindfulness practice because you start to immerse your senses in nature, and start to see the special characteristics in the forests surrounded by trees. After a while, you will be able to tune in your senses, you will be able to feel the breeze on the side of your cheeks, hear the birds sing, hear the flowing of the rivers and brooks, and even hear the trees gently move.
By tuning into your senses, you are able to reduce the volume of your inner thoughts and bring yourself into the present moment where you can appreciate what nature has to offer
Shinrin yoku isn't about hiking, it is about connection and relationships. Over time you will learn about the beauty and stillness of nature, and how it calms your mind and talks to your soul. In the Forest, monks have long relied on the solitude that

they find under the trees and in the quiet of nature on their path to enlightenment.

It is believed that when people synchronise themselves with nature, and become one with nature, then they will experience enhanced mental health.

In a research study, 71% of participants who took part in a walk through nature and forest experienced a reduction in their symptoms of depression .

When we are in nature surrounded by trees, the energy that comes from the trees has the ability to affect a person's emotional, spiritual and mental health. The energy vibrations from trees are slower, which allows them to transmit the positive energy vibes of safety, stability and security, and by resonating with the trees energy, people become more centred and grounded.

There are many physical benefits to be gained from being out in nature, and they can have quite a big positive impact on the immune system and our health:-

- Increased immune function
- Reduced blood pressure
- Reduced lung inflammation
- Improved cardiac and pulmonary function
- Improved oxidative stress and antioxidants
- Improved cardio vascular parameters
- Decreased blood glucose levels

The mental benefits of being out in nature and Shinrin Yoku include:-

- Improvement in anxiety and depression
- Improved mood
- Reduced stress
- Improved attention and cognitive capacity

The whole experience of Shinrin Yoku / Forest Bathing is to open the doors to your senses and fully engage with nature and its healing powers. Forest bathing helps your body, and mind, go into a quiet state of relaxation.

In Nature it is about listening to the sounds, looking around at the sights, and feeling the wonderful energies which are around you. Forest bathing is about reciprocity and not just taking from nature and the forest but also giving back your energy to the forest.

On your walk through the forest, it is about learning to become a partner with the forest and the trees, and listen for invitations from around you, and become one and part of nature. Take time to notice what you see, open your senses to what is around you.

There are many things you can do to become closer with the forest.

- Earth invitations:- walk barefoot, feel the dirt in your hands, explore the forest floor, look for animal tracks, find a stone and hold it and feel the connection.
- Air invitations:- breathwork in nature is wonderful to be able to connect. Try reciprocity breathing with the trees, and feel the oxygen flowing into your lungs, and the carbon dioxide being taken in by the trees, watch the clouds.
- Fire invitations:- these include speaking aloud back to the forest, talking to trees (they are good listeners) and remember we are all energy, both you and the tree and energy.
- Water invitations:- sit by water, gaze at the water, touch the water, put your feet in the stream, talk to the water.

Shinrin Yoku and being in nature is truly a wonderful way of practising mindfulness, and also connecting with nature and trees.

I know to many people who have never practised forest bathing, taking to trees and hugging trees and connecting with nature is a strange concept, but the more you are able to connect and listen to nature, the more you can feel the incredible benefits of being in nature, and the more you will feel at home and connected to everything around you.

The Scandinavian way of life

I am briefly going to go into the wonderful ways of life that have come from Scandinavian countries such as Denmark, Norway, Sweden and Finland. Year after year the Scandinavian countries always come near the top of the best places to live in the world, and there is a reason for that. And I want to quickly explore the wonderful concepts from these wonderful countries and parts of their way of live which may fit well into your own lives.

Hygge

I am sure many people have heard of the Danish way of life word of Hygge. Some words that describe Hygge would be warm, cozy, contentedness, togetherness, relaxation and comfort.

Hygge has the following principles:-

1. Mindfulness and the senses:- being in the moment. Being fully engaged in the activity that you are doing right now. Not worrying about the past, future, just being in the now. Enjoy every moment, the smell of your coffee before it touches your lips, the touch of your partners hands, the smile of your children's faces, enjoy the present moment, what is happening now and feel and sense it

2. Being grateful and positive:- stop being negative. ALWAYS look on the positive side of things. Even when negative things come along, turn them into positive. Be grateful for what you have in your life. Tell loved ones and friends you appreciate them. Talk about the good things instead of whingeing and complaining, and think positively in everything that you do.

3. Be cozy, comfortable and at ease:- surround yourself with things that are warm, comfortable and make you feel happy and at ease. Get rid of the negatives in your life, including people.

4. Nature:- we come from nature physically and spiritually, so get out into nature, connect with nature, go to the woods, beach, go on a hike.

5. Pleasure:- this is basically enjoying the simple pleasures in life. Slow down and enjoy the simple things in life. This could be something as small as watching your children, as they laugh, and have fun, or walking on the beach, find those moments and make them special. The hygge lifestyle is about experiencing what is around us. True joy and happiness lies in the little moments.

6. Togetherness:- What is the most important thing in your life? The most important thing is for you to spend quality time with the ones who mean the most to you, your children, family, parents, friends. We are all connected, and there is nothing better

than a catch up with your bestie, or playing games with friends, or snuggled up on the sofa with your partner, or the Sunday lunch at your parents. None of us live forever, so appreciate the time while people are still here, You will regret not doing when they have gone.

7. Minimalist and quiet:- we get caught up with wanting everything, and lots of things in the house, lots of clothes, and having too much stuff can be stressful, and drain your energy.

A minimalist lifestyle allows you to breathe, to relax,

The hygge way is about comfort, simple décor, cozy and comfy things to sit on and lie on in living rooms, candles instead of lights left on, cotton sheets on the bed. It is also about taking care of yourself, the bath time on your own, and time relaxing, treating yourself to new clothes or a spa day.

Hygge is about comfort, ease, togetherness and enjoying every moment with those closest to you, and living in the moment.

Lagom

Lagom is kind of the Swedish version of Hygge, and the words to describe Lagom are:- Just right – adequate – enough – sufficient – suitable – in moderation – in balance – it is just the right amount.

Lagom is very similar to Hygge, but all is good in just the right amount, family time, sleep, work, possessions, diet. It is about practising kindness, self-control, learning to slow down and not rush, getting in touch with nature.

A lovely concept in Lagom is something called 'Fika 'which basically means having that extra snack time with friends and coworkers, where it is relaxed, cozy, spending quality time together over coffee and some cake and talking about anything, Do this at home with your partner, your children, and instead of gadgets taking over, have some Fika time and reconnect.

Fruliftsliv

Friluftsliv is the Norwegian equivalent to Hygge and Lagom, and it is translated to open air living, or free air life. It is more about opening your door and reconnecting with nature, very much like Shinrin Yoku and Forest Bathing.

Just be:- it really is just about stepping outside, and breathing, and doing the following things:-sitting still in nature, smelling roses, drinking water from a river or water bottle, lying on the grass and looking up into the sky, and reconnecting, taking a nap, feeling the breeze around you, watching sunsets and sunrises, sitting their and breathing in the clean fresh air.

"If you truly love nature, you will find beauty everywhere"
Vincent Van Gogh – Artist

Go on adventures and let your mind wander, if you are up a mountain or near a ledge, peak over the edge, gaze at the moon, listen to the sounds of birds and other animals around.

Friluftsliv is about playing too, gather seashells, gather rocks, let your inner animal out, have water fights, look in rock pools for marine life, sketch and paint, take photos, make music, slide down a hill, skim stones, build a sandcastle, and enjoy life.

Life is too short not too. So have fun and connect with nature, and enjoy this time with family, friends, children.

Sometimes it is good to just forget everything and become a kid again, enjoy the simple pleasures in life, sit and watch the sun go down, play in the rain, give a tree a hug, get all your friends together and spend time out in nature, walk barefoot in the forest and in the sand on the beach, go find the end of the rainbow, skinny dip.

I think you can see from the above that there are 3 wonderful ways of life which are deep in mindfulness and living life in the present and enjoying every moment.

Now the Finnish concept doesn't need much explanation and is a fantastic way of life I think, it is called 'Kalsarikanni 'which translated means 'staying home alone and getting drunk in your underwear 'which I am sure you agree is not a bad way to relax and be in the moment.

Getting out in nature, whether it be in the forest and woods, or walking along the beach and listening to the waves, and walking barefoot in the sand, has so many health benefits, and is so incredibly beneficial for your mental health and alleviating stress.

The Viking Buddha has another book due out in 2025 which is called 'Nature's Way' which delves much deeper into nature's way, the power of trees, and the different kinds of things you can do to get the most out of being outside in nature, and also the many benefits which you will get from that walk in the woods or along the beach, or an hike up a mountain.

Chapter 17
Ho'oponopono

I would like to tell you about the wonderful ancient practice of Ho'oponopono, which has been practised for 1000s of years by people in Hawaii, and is truly a wonderful, and it is a very powerful healing process. I only go into this wonderful technique in a little detail in this book, but again on the "awakening workshop" and group sessions we cover this in greater detail.

Ho'oponopono is about the art of forgiveness. Its about solving conflicts, and setting emotions free. Ho'oponopono basically means to fix and error or mistake.

(Hawaiian) Ho'o - "cause"   pono " –perfection"

Ho'oponopono is a technique which is used to clean and erase memories that create repressing beliefs in our subconscious mind.

The aim of Ho'oponopono is find out who we really are, and see beyond all the judgements both internal and external and any shallow beliefs from others or ourselves.

So, in essence, what Ho'oponopono really does, is it searches for inner peace, and also transmutation of the past. It helps us find the divinity that lives within each of us, and it fixes errors, it cleans and brings light into us and around us.

It also helps us to re-connect, and it does that by cleaning our repressed beliefs, with our true self and the divinity.

<u>The Huna Philosophy</u>
Huna:- that which is difficult to see
Hu:- movement   Na:- calm

This philosophy was born around 5,000 years ago in Polynesia, and it encourages questioning and reflection within ourselves and others around us. It is an open technique based on the Universal truths.

The 14 Huna Principles
1. we create our own reality, through our beliefs, expectations, and fears.
2. We get that which we focus on.
3. We are responsible for our own experience.
4. Thoughts attract their equivalent
5. Life presents you the content of all your thoughts.
6. When you change your way of thinking, your life experience changes.
7. You are an unlimited being, Everything is possible. You just need to believe it.
8. The present is the fruit of the past and the seed of the future.
9. The world is what you think it is. If you change your beliefs, the world around you changes.
10. The energy flow to the place where your attention is directed.
11. Nothing happens that we haven't attracted first.
12. All power comes from within
13. We create exactly what is related to our vibration
14. Think about what you wish for. Thoughts are vibrations.

7 Huna principles which will change your life
- IKE:- the world is what you think it is
- KALA:- There are no limits, everything is possible
- MAKIA:- energy flows where the attention goes
- MANAWA:- now is the moment of power
- ALOHA:- to love is to be happy with
- MANA:- all power comes from within
- PONO:- effectiveness is the measure of truth

The Meaning of Aloha
- A:- AO – means light. We need to make sure we always have positive intentions and our behaviour is pure and moves us towards the light.
- L:- LOKAHI – means Oneness. All is one. Support people who are on the path with us. Oneness means we have to be PONO and ONE with everybody.

- O:- OIAIO – means Truth. Tell the truth. Many of us are too polite to tell the truth, and we don't participate completely in the process in the construction of our universe. Don't withhold your feelings, as this doesn't allow us to be one with the people around us.
- H:- HA'A HA'A:- means to be Humble. Let go of your ego. If you play the game of power, you will always have to know more than others. Let go of your ego… Share with others, remain humble.
- A:- ALOHA – means Absolute, True Love. don't think you are better than anyone else, don't make comparisons, judgements etc, because when you do, you separate yourself from true love.

To find ABSOLUTE TRUE LOVE, you need to be HUMBLE, and tell the TRUTH, which allows you to reach ONENESS with yourself and everyone around you, and this will guide you to the LIGHT.

I want to tell you a story about Dr Hew Len who was a student of Mornah Simeona the creator of Self-I-Dentity through Ho'oponopono.

Between 1984 to 1987 he worked as a staff psychologist for Hawaii State Hospital where he oversaw a high security unit with male criminally insane patients. In 1987, the daily violence which once happened had virtually ceased, and these inmates were even going on off site activities. The spirit and order in the unit was so greatly improved. According to Dr Hew Len he did not do any therapy or counselling with the patients, what he did do was practice Ho'oponopono on a daily basis that included accepting 100% responsibility for everything being experienced by HIM.

Dr Hew Len said "I didn't heal them, I healed part of myself that created them"

You are 100% responsible for everything! Everything and everywhere… that means the things you do wrong, personal successes etc, but also it means if someone somewhere else did something, and you become aware of it, YOU are 100% responsible for that!

"when you return back to your inner nature – to zero – everything becomes available to you effortlessly and you are being driven by inspiration from divinity and not petty ego" Joe Vitalle

I would highly recommend getting the book 'Zero Limits' by Joe Vitale, which is a fantastic book.

So, how do we get to this magical state? It is achieved by a cleaning process which you do constantly. You clean yourself from all the subconscious garbage, the programs that run your life.

The 4 healing words of Ho'oponopono

The actual cleaning process consists of repetitions of these 4 wonderful phrases.

- I am sorry
- Please forgive me
- Thank you
- I love you

When you repeat these 4 phrases, the cleaning process just happens. You can clean relationships, people, places, life situations etc. When something comes into your awareness, you accept 100% responsibility for that thought and repeat the cleaning process.

You may ask the questions.. How can you heal yourself and others by saying these 4 phrases? Why would repeating these 4 phrases affect anything or anybody out there?

The fact is, there isn't an out there… everything happens to you, in YOUR mind.

Every single thing you see and hear, every single person you meet, you experience in your mind. You only think it is out there, and you think that absolves you from responsibility.

But actually YOU are responsible for every single thing you think, and every single thing that comes to YOUR attention. Even things you hear about while watching the news, is YOUR responsibility. This may sound a little crazy to some, and harsh to others, but realising this also means that you are also able to clear it, clean it, and through the use of these 4 phrases and forgiveness, change it.

When you are repeating these 4 phrases, you don't need anyone else to be there with you, you don't need anyone to hear you ,and you can say the words in your head, because the power is actually in the feeling and also the willingness of the universe to forgive and love. Remember we are all energy, and we are all one:-

1. I'm Sorry:- repentance – you are responsible for everything in your head, even when it is 'out there'. Once we realise we cause our own reality, we feel a natural state of remorse. So who are we asking? We ask ourselves, we are responsible for our problems, and also our forgiveness.

2. Please forgive me:- ask forgiveness – it doesn't matter who you are asking, just ask please forgive me and mean it.

3. Thank You:- gratitude – again it doesn't matter who we thank, when you are offering gratitude you are affecting your soul which is connected to the souls of all, of everyone. Thank yourself for the courage to change and learn. Thank the people who surround you.

4. I love you:- Love – say this often, and say it to all who surround you. Remember now you have no enemies around you, there is only you! You can love everything with complete honesty, because you have released all the layers of pain, anger, remorse, guilt that kept you from love.

Ho'oponopono is a wonderful practice and therapeutic technique, which I use on a daily basis, and it brings you such peace and it can be such a powerful healing tool.

Chapter 18
Neuroplasticity

How does it work?

Every task requires Neurons. A neuron is a specialised cell that transmits nerve impulses. We have these in our brain, and even the smallest task requires a vast amount of interconnected neurons. More complexed tasks require more neurons.

"Neurons that fire together, wire together"
Donald Hebb

We form new neural pathways through repetition. So, by doing things again and again, our neurons connect.

It is kind of like a dance... it takes constant repetition for neuroplasticity to work. Through repetition, they are slowly becoming connected together.

When you repeat actions, neurons wire together, and fire together. You need to keep repeating these actions.

Stage 1:- Chemical changes
When do chemical changes happen? Chemical changes include the following:-
- Neurons which carry signals to the brain are destroyed
- Signals transmitted between brain cells, carried between synapses by neurotransmitters are interrupted.
- The connections between nerve cells of the brain become interrupted.

The chemical changes are only temporary, they do not last forever. What you need to do in the short term is to repeat actions to experience chemical changes.

Stage 2:- Structural changes
Structural changes last longer. The brain structure can change as we learn and form new habits. When the neurons bind together the wire together, and there is a change in the brain structure. The brain structure also changes as we age. We notice certain degenerative factors occur when we get older.

In order to change your brain structure, you need constant repetition that often takes years of practice. By training your brain on a constant basis, you can improve brain structure and cognition. Your brain structures around your lifestyle.

Stage 3:- Functional changes.
This means the brain has changed. The brain functions are optimised. Now there are different abilities that weren't present before, which have now been acquired, and there is a huge increase in neurological performance.

So, if you want to use neuroplasticity to strengthen things that are weak within your mind, such as your memory, or physical co-ordination, you need to alter your brain and form these new connections. You can literally change anything in your life, by forming these new connections.

You need to self-audit yourself, and figure out the things you don't do very well. You need to discover your strengths, but also your weaknesses. Then find specific activities and exercises for those weaknesses.

Improve overall memory
Repeat things constantly for long term memory. You need to learn how to move things from your short-term memory to your long-term memory. And this is done by repetition.

If you have a few things that you need to remember, make a story about the things you want to remember.

The grey matter in your brain contains most of the brain's neuronal cell bodies. The grey matter includes regions of the brain involved in muscle control, and sensory perception such as seeing and hearing, memory, emotions, speech decision making and self-control.

The proportion of grey matter can change, and synapses may strengthen or weaken over time.

Until the end of the 20th century scientists assumed that grey matter could never increase in adults, but now recent research has found that this is not true.

Elderly people do show decreased grey matter in the brain, but when it comes to neuroplasticity, we look at things in a different way. Every single person can change their brain, and neural structure through the concept of plasticity.

So, research has shown that a lot of different aspects of the brain can be altered even through adulthood, and neuroplasticity can be observed from multiple scales, from microscopic changes in individual neurons, to larger scale changes such as cortical remapping in response to injury.

"Neurons that fire together, wire together... Neurons that fire out of sync, fail to link"

Each time we learn a new dance step, it reflects a change in our physical brains, new wires (neural pathways) that give instructions to our bodies on how to perform the step.

When you stop exercising, it reflects changes in our physical brain as well, old wires that give instructions related to physical activities weaken or disappear.

If you start a new hobby, and you stop every week, only to get back to doing it after 2 weeks, and you repeat, you will most likely never wire it properly in your brain.

There is a misconception that childhood and young adulthood are the peak periods for brain growth, and in older adulthood, it is considered as a period of cognitive decline. This is not true. Recent research has shown that under the right circumstances, the power of brain plasticity can help adult minds grow.

Neuroplasticity actually enables people to recover from many things such as strokes, injury, birth abnormalities, and can improve symptoms of autism, ADHD, learning disabilities and other brain deficits.

It can also help with depression, addictions and reverse obsessive compulsive patterns.

The brain has the ability to change, adapt and adjust, both physically, functionally, and chemically, by stimulation from your environment, behaviour, thinking, emotions, habits, and other physical elements.

Neural chains and connections are not fixed at all. When we practice one activity on a consistent basis, neuronal circuits are being formed, leading to better ability to form the practical task with less waste of energy.

Once we stop practicing a certain activity, the brain will redirect those neuronal circuits through a much known 'use it or lose it 'principle.

You have the ability to rewire your brain, we aren't just talking about thoughts, we are talking about changing the actual chemistry and physical state of your brain.

Neuroplasticity and Mental Health

How much can neuroplasticity affect our mental health?

Schizophrenia, Bipolar disorder, depression, OCD, and phobic behaviours, epilepsy, occur because of neuroplasticity changes in the brain.

The Mental illnesses are due to a chemical change, and as a result, mental illnesses are part of neuroplasticity., because of these behaviours, your brain is changing its chemistry, and the more this behaviour is repeated, the more it is going to become wired in your brain, and the more it will be hard for you to get over it.

If there is a behaviour that is related to mental health illnesses, that is not treated properly, or is not met by an equivalent that can actually reduce its impact, it will become stronger and stronger every single day.

What we want to achieve, is to build something else in your brain, to use your brains plasticity to build another system that can work on lowering the impact of a certain mental health illness that you have. It can even get to a point that you have full control over it, by just having some triggers and cues that you use, then you can get yourself out of this mental health state at any time.

It is possible to overcome a mental health condition such as depression, schizophrenia, bipolar, addiction, by driving a brain back towards normal operation through neuroplastic change.

Here is what you can do...

- Introspection:- become aware of the problems, how they occur, their effect on you and your surroundings
- Exercises:- practices and exercises to help you overcome the problem by finding a fix for it
- Repetition:- neuroplasticity is all about repetition. make sure that you repeat the exercises daily and regularly to change and help heal your mental health issues.

Every day your brain is like an old tape recorder, playing your problems the moment you wake up, which are connected to certain memories, which in turn are connected to certain people, places and things. So this is the record of the past, and when you start your day like this, you are already thinking and living in the past.

Our memories are emotions which are the outcome and product of past experiences. When you recall your problems, you feel sad, unhappy, and pain, and this creates your state of being, and if you start your day with your past, then sooner or later that past and thoughts will become your future.

Every one of your thoughts, have something to do with your destiny. Think negative thoughts and that is what your future looks like, think positive thoughts, then your future will be more positive. If you keep thinking in the past, you are going to keep creating the same life for yourself.

This normally happens because every day we do the same things, the same procedures, we get out of bed, we look at our phones and social media, watch the news on TV, coffee in same cup, take a shower, and do everything the same way nearly every day.

When you get to work you see the same people, and some of them will irritate you, and push the same buttons every single day, and in the evening, you go back home, and have the same routine nearly every single night, and the repeat, and it becomes your routine. And then it becomes a subconscious program.

By the time we are 35 years old, 95% of who we are is a memorised set of behaviours, emotional reactions, unconscious habits, perceptions, beliefs and attitudes that are hardwired that are just like a program.

With the other 5% of your conscious mind, you might be saying I want to be happy, healthy, wealthy, etc, but unfortunately your body is run by the subconscious minds 95%.

Most people spend around 70% of their lives in survival mode just going along with their safe lives and waiting for something to happen, and all they do is choose the negative things instead of the infinite possibilities available to them in the quantum field.

Your brain produces the same chemistry each and every time you recall negative events and experiences as if it is happening again. You are sending these same signals to your body about these negative events, and your body thinks it is happening right now, and that is why people are constantly reliving their negative states because they are constantly thinking about them.

Unfortunately your body becomes programmed to this negative programming, and even though you want to change, the body doesn't like this, as this is stepping into the unknown, and this is why the body would rather feel suffering, guilt and hurt because it feels familiar and safe and it can predict it.

The best ways to bypass this negative programming, is by meditation, imagery and visualisation. hypnosis, affirmations etc. it is about repetition, and teaching the mind to accept change, and allow your body to feel emotions of your thoughts, and this is where you can download your new programming, and new future life.

On average each person has about 60,000 to 70,000 thoughts in one day. 90% of those thoughts are the same thoughts as the day before. Just because you have a thought it doesn't mean that it is true.

You have the power to change your life anytime you want, You can change your brains neuroplasticity and change it to whatever you want in life.

Chapter 19
Quantum Embodiment

FACT:- Everything you see around you is made up of space (atoms) and time. Space and matter is made up of atoms.

Did you know there are 7 billion billion atoms per person, that's 7,000,000,000,000,000,000 per person, and those atoms are not as solid as we think they are.
Actually, each atom is mostly empty space. All matter is simply a collection of atoms. Everything is made of atoms, and all atoms are made of energy pockets. Matter is energy. Every single thing is made of energy, and these strings of energy all vibrate at different frequencies.

"Inside atoms there are even tinier bits of matter, including protons and neutrons, which are made of smaller particles called quarks, but physicists realise that this might not quite be the end of the line, and these subatomic bits might be actually made up of something even smaller. Tiny vibrating strands, or loops of energy called strings. Everything that exists is made up of this one kind of ingredient. Strings can take on different properties depending on how they vibrate, creating many kinds of particles". Brian Greene

Energy can be in more than one place at a time. Energy appears in response to thought, to mind. It is YOUR mind that chooses to see a thing, and in response to that intent or thought, the energy of that thing, turns up where your mind decides to see it.
Energy is a wave that exists all across spacetime, and when your mind chooses to see a thing at a particular place and time, that wave collapses into a particle. Once the mind withdraws, the particle becomes a wave once again.

"In the quantum world, there is a sense in which things don't like to be tied down to just one location, or to follow just one path. It's almost as if things were in more than one place at a time. And what you do there, can have an immediate effect somewhere else, even if there is nobody there" Brain Greene

Everything already exists as a probability when spread across space and time. When you choose to observe it, you then cause it to be a definite thing. Energy is both a wave and a particle. Energy pulses in and out of existence an estimated 50 billion times a second. This is what enables change to happen, when you think about the Law of Attraction.

It seems that energy rearranges or arranges itself according to the information that is filled around. Once the information changes, the arrangement changes.

Think of information as thoughts or beliefs. In essence, you have 50 billion chances per second, to change who you are, or to change the circumstances in your life. The minute you change your mind, the universe changes to that degree.

Thought shapes energy, therefore thought literally shapes matter.

"Every possibility happens, but in an alternate reality. Some physicists believe that all of the possibilities that exist in the quantum world, they never go away. But, Instead, each and every possible outcome actually happens, only most of them happen in other universes, parallel to our own"

Physical reality is a hologram, a projection, an illusion.

We actually see less than $1/50^{th}$ of 1% of what is out there, but we believe that what we see is all that is real, we discount what we don't see. In other words, we are given 100 billion bits per second, but we reject all but 2000 bits per second – the same 2000 over and over again, due to our beliefs and attachments.

Time is also an illusion. All moments of time already exist simultaneously. The only reality is now!

So, what does quantum energy have to do with money and anything else? Consciousness + thought = reality experience.

Quantum physics shows how we are all connected, and how we are all one being, that perpetuates an illusion of separate individual beings.

Your body is made up cells, these cells are in turn made up of molecules, which are in turn made up of atoms, which in turn are made up subatomic particles such as electrons – this is the world of quantum physics.

Quantum energy is NOT 3 dimensional, not linear, not mechanical. It is multi-dimensional, uncountable and unbound by space and time.

So, what is your body actually made of? Tissues and organs. What are tissues and organs made up of? Cells. What are cells made of? Molecules. What are molecules made of? Atoms. What are atoms made up of? Subatomic particles. What are subatomic particles made up of? ENERGY. They are energy.

Things appear "solid" because that is how human senses and density is built. - but really nothing is solid.

No solid object is solid. It is made up of rapidly flashing packets of energy, billions and trillions of packets of energy, which flash in, and flash out of that space where the object is

"So why does a human body or a car look like a solid continuous object? It is actually a rapidly flashing field of energy. The world is a rapid flash that causes an illusion of being solid and continuous. No matter is a wholly independent existence, independent of the observer. As some scientists say, if everyone, and everything in the universe stopped looking at the moon, and thinking about it, it would not be a physical moon anymore, it would be a probability of existence. The act of observation make the probability become a definite thing, and all other probabilities of it being elsewhere in the same world a non-existence. Continuous attention keeps it that way, producing the illusion of a solid continuous existence"

David Gikandi

Quantum energy is intelligent, it isn't dead, it is living. Quantum particles make decisions, they are powered by intelligence, and not only that but they also know instantly what decisions are being made by other particles anywhere else in the universe.

This synchronicity across space and time is instantaneous, they communicate without taking any time.

You are the cause for everything around you. Nothing you observe can exist without your observation. All you need to do is choose what you wish to observe, choose it with certainty, and with consistency, and this will cause it to materialise over time.

Your perception is just an optical illusion. Our perception creates our reality based on how we judge and process the events in our lives.

"People only see what they are prepared to see"
Ralph Waldo Emerson

The world as we perceive it, is constantly shifting and constantly changing according to our beliefs and the decisions that we make, not only about the world, but about ourselves.

Whatever environment we have come from, whatever family we have come from, and whatever experiences we have had, we view from those lenses, so everything becomes a reality based on from where we have come from the past.

Whatever you are perceiving, is creating your reality.

In the experiencing of many of our lives, this is a Newtonian experience, because we may all be made of quantum particles, but in this experiencing, at this moment, they are very densely packed, and car running into you will HURT, if you step out in front of it.

Your perception gives you the experience you are having, you are living your reality through your thoughts.

"We don't see things as they are. We see them as we are"
Anais Nin

"The reality that you perceive right here is an outward projection of your internal state" Joe Vitale

The world is not being done to you, it is being done by you. It is not coming at you, it is coming FROM you

"Atoms are not things, they are only tendencies"
Werner Heisenberg

"You are not here to create something outside of you, you are here to find who you are, and express that outside of you".
Amir Zoghi

Chapter 20
Epigenetics

Did you know that we all have the ability to change the expression of our genes?

Your DNA and chromatine regulate the expression of your genes, they can be altered by either external – environmental, or internal-mental and emotional signals without altering the gene sequence itself.

The food you eat, the lifestyle you maintain, the stress, the dramas, the emotional experience, and the quality of the thoughts that you think, and also the relationships that you have, each send signals at different vibrational levels that either support cellular growth, optimal functioning, or predispose you to illness and disease.

Genes are NOT your destiny, as they can be switched on or off. What you need to understand, is that with your thoughts and actions you can build and reinforce new neural networks in your brain, which then send this information to your endocrine system, which in turn send new signals to the receptors on the cells. The receptors on the cells absorb the quality of the vibration being received.

We distribute and produce billions of volts of energy every single second. This is circulated through the body and through the space creating intersecting fields.

Joining us at birth, we have an amazing partner in our existence, our microbiome. These are micro-organisms such as bacteria, fungi and viruses that cover our skin, and are in our mouth, fill out stomach and other body parts, sharing their DNA and interacting with ours.

You can heal all of your chronic, emotional, mental and physical illnesses and disorders by learning how to redirect your genes, and to shift your DNA's expression, and to optimise your health and wellness, and improve your existence and the way that you feel, whilst learning how to control your body's biochemical production.

You can become an active participant in your own healing, your emotional and spiritual growth, and also prevention of future illnesses. The genes in each cell's DNA respond to the signals that they receive from the environment, externally and internally. You can turn the expressions of your genes on or off.

The food you eat, the company you keep, the TV you watch, the books you read, each of them changes your chemistry and determines the wellness that you experience.

Every experience and interaction you have, good or bad, send coded messages to your brain, your cells, to either feel safe and relaxed, or to feel stressed. This establishes your emotional state, which is them expressed through your thoughts, which in turn creates an environment where you either feel safe or unsafe.

The thoughts that you have, send electrical impulses about the way you are perceiving and evaluating the world, and those signals send codes of the judgements that you have about your environment, through your nervous system. All of this produces the results you experience, and this triggers the biological response and emotional response, and this happens thousands of times every day on a subconscious level.

Your beliefs build your ego identity, and this influences your gene expression. Your thoughts and your actions direct your cells on how to respond, the receptors receive these signals, and send these signals to the nucleus within each cell and then based on the vibrational energy, it produces the bio chemicals to maintain survival.

It is you who chooses how you look at life, and each choice influences your health.

Whether your thoughts and actions are good or bad, they impact your brains receptors, this changes your DNA and cells.

Every single moment you are receiving signals from around you, and from inside yourself and your thoughts. These are either positive or negative, which influence you. It is so vitally important to send the positive vibrations to your DNA and cells.

We need to learn how to switch on the vibrations, thoughts and feelings which bring you empowerment, and joy, which recode your cells and DNA, instead of negatives, which bring on illness and disease.

The roots of any condition you may be suffering from are buried in the unconscious mind and body. Any weakness, or pain which we feel physically has a mental or emotional history which needs to be looked at, and dealt with. Your body is giving you messages from the depth of your being, to pay attention and do something about what is causing these issues.

You need to deal with past hurt, past trauma, and you need to go past the walls which have been built in your life, which are saying avoid, don't deal with me, and you need to look within, and deal with them right now.

Whatever has happened in the past is over, but until you deal with it, it is still deeply ingrained in you, and your unconscious mind, and is holding you back and making you sick.

Why are you still carrying around the fear, the trauma, the hurt, the pain? Because if you are holding onto all of this negative energy and blockages, that can, and most probably is, the cause of your cancer, your heart disease, your diabetes, and of any other type of imbalance in your endocrine system, because that part of your unconscious mind and body is still holding onto all of these negative emotions and causing blockages in your body, which along with other lifestyle choices eventually cause dis-ease.

The Chinese and eastern medicine looks at illness as an interference of circulation. All of the hormones, the neurotransmitters, are being interfered with and creates blockages and back up in your body, and these need unblocking by facing these problems, and dealing with problems of the past.

Anger and stress deposits that we make throughout our lives are put in a bank account, and if they aren't withdrawn, this becomes the build-up of blockages and rage within our body that eventually erupt into symptoms within the body.

What we repress inside and are unwilling to look at within our minds, are the things that eventually make us sick and harm us.

If you ever want to get deeper into the subject of epigenetics, I would suggest watching videos or buying books written by the absolutely brilliant Bruce Lipton. Here are a few quotes from him about epigenetics.

"I will show you the science of how the cells actually work, and you will have more knowledge than most doctors in the world today, because they still believe in the genes" Bruce Lipton

"What can cause dis-ease?, either the protein is bad, or the signal is bad. People with bad proteins got them from birth defects, because if you were born with defective genes, and the genes make the protein, then the protein is defective. But less than 5% of the world population has birth defects. That means 95% of the people should have a healthy existence, but if you are one of the healthy people and now you are sick, what would cause the problem?
There are only 3 ways to mess up the signal – 1. Trauma... 2. Toxins... both of these interfere with the propagation of the signal...
and 3. Thoughts – the mind... there is nothing wrong with the body, it is just sending the wrong signal at the wrong time, so if you change your thought and your mind, you can change the biology" Dr Bruce Lipton

"the mind is the primary cause of illness on our planet today. Perception is name of the switch that controls your biology. It is you and how you see the world that controls the biology" Dr Bruce Lipton

Your genes don't make the decisions! A gene is just a blueprint. The gene has no control. The gene is never off or on. What controls the signal? Perception. Your thoughts.

"you are not the victim of your genes, because you control your genes. One gene blueprint using epigenetic control, can make 30,000 different proteins from one blueprint. So you can come with good genes, and then through epigenetic control create cancer, diabetes, heart disease, and it has nothing to do

with the genes, but epigenetic control, it returns responsibility for your health to YOU" Dr Bruce Lipton

"95% of cancer is not because of mutant genes, but because of epigenetic control. And it can be passed from parent to child like genes, but the difference is you can change your epigenetics at any time... if you change your perception, your thoughts, you change the reading of your genes" Dr Bruce Lipton

If a doctor tells you that you have a disease, and you believe that, then you can create the disease.

"when you look at yourself, you are not a single entity, but you are a community of 50 trillion cells. Every cell is intelligent, but when they are in a community, they give up their personal intelligence, and respond to the central voice, and if the central voice says to die, the cells will die. The central voice is THE MIND. There are signals from the environment, both the internal and external environment, and the function of the brain is to receive the signals, and then interpret those signals and then send the information to the cells to control the behaviour and the genetics" Dr Bruce Lipton

"The function of the brain is perception, and from that creates the mind. The placebo effect is when you have a very positive thought, that something can heal you, even if it is a sugar pill, but you believe that it is real medicine, then you can heal yourself, The pill didn't heal you, it was the thought that healed you" Dr Bruce Lipton

Statistics show that 33.3% of all medical healings including surgery are from the placebo effect.

"negative effect is called the 'nocebo effect' and in the same power that positive thinking can heal you, negative thinking can kill you. The point is that negative thinking can create all the effects of chemotherapy. If a doctor tells you that you have a disease, or the doctors tells you that you are going to die, and

YOU believe the doctor because he is a professional, the belief will give you a disease and can cause you to die, so belief becomes an important part of medicine" Dr. Bruce Lipton

One of the most important reasons we get sick is due to stress.

"the functions of the stress hormones is to take the energy of the body and get it all to run and fight, so the stress hormones will shut off the functions of things that will not be needed in fight or flight. One of the most important uses of energy in the body is the immune system. Stress hormones shut off the immune system, and the significance is, that every one of you right now is infected with almost all of the disease germs that humans have. You all have viruses, bacteria and parasites in your body right now. If your immune system is working properly, it will suppress these parasites, germs, viruses etc, but the moment you start to shut off the immune system then these organisms begin to start growing again" Bruce Lipton

So it is NOT true that you catch a disease, you already have the disease.

"The medical people call these germs and parasites opportunistic organisms, so if you are under stress and you shut off the immune system, then you give these organisms the opportunity to them make the disease"
Dr Bruce Lipton

To end this chapter, You need to start changing your perception and thoughts. You can heal yourself from any disease or condition by changing your thoughts to positive ones, and thus changing your cells instructions and blueprint inside your body.

It doesn't matter if you have diabetes, heart disease or stage 4 cancer, you can change your life and regain your health at any time you want to, by changing your thoughts, perception, and thinking positive thoughts and most importantly not getting stressed. You need to deal with trauma, and learn how to not get stressed over things, and learn to change your thoughts and perceptions to renew your cells into new healthy cells and a new healthy blueprint inside your mind and body.

Chapter 21
The Enneagram

In this chapter, I want to provide a brief overview of this really interesting personality type profiling called The Enneagram.

The Enneagram is an important resource for people to understand why they are the way they are.

There are 9 different personality types with are found within the Enneagram, which shows dominant behaviours, motivations and fears, but also has other variations which are based on their life, and positive and negative traits.

Each type has its main characteristics, but also 2 different wings, and 3 different subtypes.

This is a brief breakdown of the different types, and if you want to learn more about the enneagrams we do go further into this in our 3 day workshop also called "The Awakening"

So here we go with the different types:-

Type 1:- The Performer / Perfectionist / Idealistic one
- Principled, purposeful, self-controlled, morally sound, conscientious, advocates for justice, passionate about being right, and balanced in choices. Chase knowledge and wisdom and seek approval.
- They acknowledge feelings of anger, but as they don't want to express anger they hold it in.
- Most important thing is improving themselves and the world
- They want to be right, perfect and good. Strong sense of right and wrong. Strong sense of purpose.
- They will often have tight bodies, and rigid and tense with stiff upright bodies. They seem hypervigilant. They can be experienced by others as judgemental and critical.
- They have a strong moral code, but they find it difficult to receive anger or criticism. They try to keep their flaws hidden and suppressed.

- They are hard workers but can use alcohol to loosen up as it can be difficult for this type to be spontaneous and have fun.
- They will often have high ideas and expectations to match. They believe their way is the only way.
- Their vision drives them to perfection, and there is a tendency to go over the top in all aspects of life.
- They worry about making mistakes and others judging them
- Work and career:- they like precision, so make good judges, quality managers, auditors, accountants, architects, school teachers. They are natural leaders but may micromanage.
- Continuum:- lower:- self-righteous, punitive, OCD, explosive, extreme guilt... middle:- Opinionated, preachy, disciplined, self-critical... higher:- discerning, open, wise, still ego based... liberated:- know all is fine as it is, both perfection and imperfection.
- Famous type 1s:- Julie Andrews, Margaret Thatcher, Steve Jobs, Al Gore, CS Lewis, Michelle Obama, Martin Luther King, Judge Judy, Malcolm X, Meryl Streep.

Type 2:- The Nurturer / The Caregiver / The Empath
- Type 2's are generous, very friendly and warm. They are people pleasers and they easily understand the needs of others. But they seek acceptance and love from others
- Attentive to the needs of others around them. They care very deeply and sometimes put their needs last.
- They have a fear of being unwanted or unneeded, and the most important thing for this type is feeling love and feeling connected.
- Self-confident, haughty, charismatic and intense
- They are usually upbeat, positive, sweet, gushy, lots of energy.
- Some of their positivity comes from denying their own issues, needs and problems.
- They have belief that having their own needs is unattractive and will push people away.
- They sometimes feel like needs not being met in primary relationships, feel lost

- They get their sense of self from connection to others.
- People are really drawn to them, they enjoy their generosity.
- They fear rejection and being taken advantage of as they have a good nature.
- At times they will feel they have given enough and will withdraw.
- They work hard to make others feel good, and usually see the glass half full, and always go the extra mile.
- Work and career:- they will look for a career where there is a connection to others. Entertainers, therapists, event planners, receptionists, hospitality, nurses.
- Continuum:- lower:- victim, manipulative, entitled, angry... Middle:- displaced anger, self-important, intrusive, pleasers and advice givers... Higher:- empathetic, unconditional love, able to be direct, still ego based... liberated:- love is inherent.
- Famous type 2s:- Dolly Parton, Debbie Reynolds, Lewis Carroll, Doris Day, Nancy Reagan, Yoko Ono, Barry Manilow, Stevie Wonder.

Type 3:- The Achievier / The Pragmatist /The Performer

- They are drivers, competitive, image conscious, goal driven
- Regularly set goals, and work very hard to achieve them
- Success is a driving factor, and they have a fear of being unworthy
- They seek validation and acceptance through their success.
- High energy and focus on personal development and being valued is the most important.
- They can be excessively well groomed, not an hair out of place, nails colour coordinated etc.
- Their talking style is controlled, logical, abrasive, sharp, loud.

- They have easy access to emotions such as anger, annoyance, irritation, resentment, and all other emotions are blocked, they find emotions annoying.
- Generally they are not really interested in feelings of others such as pain and suffering, and show a lack of compassion, and come across as cold and superficial.
- Everything is used for success, friendships, marriages, business, education, homes, clothing, and there is an underlying connection to what is going to make them appear, feel and experience success.
- When you are useful to them, they will treat you as valuable, if you lose that value then you are expendable.
- They want to be at the top of their field, the most confident, the best, and they use their image to try and get love, and whatever is required for this end is done.
- People are attracted to their personality because they appear sparkly and because of their positivity, but then find they lack depth and compassion.
- They want to excel in every aspect of life, but they need to be rewarded for their accomplishments.
- They do whatever it takes to be successful and get results.
- Work and career:- they are all about work and success. Often managers and leaders, investments, sales, advertising, law, police, medicine,
- Continuum:- Lower:- revengeful, deceitful, success... Middle:- grandiose, image obsessed, over achievers, cool, abrasive... Higher:- self-improving, authentic, other interests and real relationships, still ego based...Liberated:- know inherent love and value
- Famous 3s:- Will Smith, Dwayne (The Rock) Johnson, Oprah Winfrey, Justin Bieber, Muhammed Ali, Lady Gaga, Beyonce, Tony Blair, Sharon Stone, Tiger Woods

Type 4:- The Individualist / Romantic / Creative

- This type is expressive, dramatic, temperamental, self-absorbed, and introverts
- They seem their own identity to be unique among others and want to leave a lasting impression on the world.
- Have a fear of having no significance, they are very artistic.
- They don't like large groups
- They need to feel loved. They search outside of themselves to find this love, believing if they are special and unique enough they will attract love to them.
- They sometimes have an unusual style of dress and general appearance. Striking hairstyles, they are natural and authentic.
- Their talking style oozes emotion and they are sexy and sensual.
- They sometimes seem sad even when they are happy.
- They want attention and use emotion to get it. They often feel misunderstood, unnoticed, and unappreciated.
- They often feel different from others, sometimes inferior, always special.
- They often isolate, then feel lonely and abandoned. Tragedy can become their identity.
- Type 4s seem to have less energy than others, feel weighted and sensitive, and cant handle as much as others. Being ordinary is the most dreadful thing, having an ordinary job is like a death sentence.
- They like to have fun, and be spontaneous
- Because of their creativity, they find day to day life difficult and even boring, and live for life's special moments.
- They don't hold back from their inner exploration. They want to live out a romantic, idealised life and life is emotional. They are committed to the highs and lows of emotions.

- They are empathetic, expressive, emotional, engaging, entertaining, unique and original.
- Work and career:- musicians, writers, actors, substitute teachers, entrepreneurs, professors, art teachers, psychotherapists, counsellors.
- Continuum:- lower:- self-destructive, suicidal, depressed, alienated, rejected… middle:- pretentious, self-centred, melancholy, isolating… higher:- creative, sensitive, self-aware, joyful, self-supporting, still ego driven… liberated:- everyone is special and ordinary
- Famous 4s:- Taylor Swift, Kate Winslet, Gene Wilder, Anne Frank, Winona Ryder, Johnny Depp, Bob Dylan, Michael Jackson

<u>Type 5:- The Investigator / The Pioneer / The Thinker</u>
- Perceptive, independent, intelligent, they seek knowledge, and deeper understanding of life.
- They enjoy alone time, and guard themselves in their emotions.
- Very curious and observant in the environments they are in.
- They are often fragile, sensitive, insignificant and frail and don't take up too much space in the world. The world is sometimes overwhelming for them, and retreat into their minds.
- They tend to be extremely quiet, isolate, and gather information to feel safe.
- They might dress goth, lots tattoos, or wear clothes that are drab and unstylish.
- They don't need to please anyone or follow any rules. They love to gather information and safe place is their mind.
- Some type 5s create mental worlds inside of their mind and fantasy worlds.
- Type 5s love learning and feel the need to understand how things work and to unravel cause and effect. They often see themselves as observers of life. Very reflective, analytical, scientific or technical.

- They are innovative, creative, independent thinkers, and they do not need other people and are self-sufficient, they don't require approval from others.
- They rarely participate in small talk, but the big ideas in life they are more interested in.
- They are protective of their own space and private with their emotions.
- Work and career:- authors / writers, data analysts, technology, data gathering, hard sciences, research, development, art and science museums etc
- Continuum:- lower:- suicidal, paranoid, antisocial... Middle:- bizarre beliefs, detached, invisible, offended when overlooked... higher:- original ideas, perceptive, competent, clear mind, share simply... Liberated:- live openly and fully.
- Famous 5s:- Bill Gates, Albert Einstein, Mark Zuckerberg, Jane Austen, Tim Burton, Alfred Hitchcock, Stephen Hawking, Agatha Christie, Stephen King, JK Rowling.

Type 6:- The Loyalist / Security Orientated / Most Reliable

- Responsible, engaging, loyal, reliable, they seek security and stability from others. They have a fear of losing their support system. They work hard and act responsibly.
- The like to feel safe, hyper vigilant, active pressured mind, fast speech
- Experience fear from thoughts, plan for scary situations. Cut off from emotion and gut
- They use rationalisation and intellectualisation.
- They are normally trustworthy, honest and loyal, they are likeable
- They are often prepared for a worst case scenario. Their focus is on problem solving, and there is sometimes a distinct lack of trust in others.
- Type 6s are all about preparation, even their contingency plans have contingency plans. They live in a hyper-arousal state of adrenaline and look for certainty in life
- They are happy to offer advice and support when needed.
- They are team players, they can be competitive but they like mutual support and cooperation from others.

- Work and career:- problem solver careers, accident investigators, pathology, detective work, police, paramedics, military.
- Continuum:- lower:- self-punishing, paranoid, lack of self-trust, drug abuse… middle:- antiauthoritarian, indecisive, defensive, loyal, dutiful… higher:- cooperative, self-reliant, healthy relationships, trust gut, still ego based…Liberated:- relaxed, open and curious
- Famous 6s:- Ben Affleck, Joe Biden, Princess Diana, David Letterman, Tom Hanks, Johnny Carson, Sigmund Freud, Chris Rock, Sarah Jessica Parker.

Type 7:- The Optimist / The Enthusiast/ The adventurer
- Adventurous, spontaneous, versatile, fun loving, optimistic.
- Fear missing out on things, enjoy being around people in social environment.
- They are prone to addictions
- Most important thing for them is to be excited about life. Enthusiasm is a must. They go through life grabbing at experience, but are trying to find what is missing unconsciously.
- They are often bouncy, energetic, wiry, athletic, lots of energy, uncomfortable with negativity.
- They don't like dark emotions and remove themselves from this type of energy
- Love to entertain, centre of attention, lift people's moods, funny, sarcastic, witty, like deep conversation if it isn't negative. Avoid all sadness and fear, and get angry when they feel trapped.
- Intellectual, try to live in the moment, life is what you make it.
- Work and career:- entertainment, travel, comedians, musicians, entrepreneurs, work in different careers trying out new ones

- Continuum:- lower:- overwhelmed, manic, explosive, escaping... Middle:- excessive, distracted, restless, enthusiastic, entertaining... Higher:- practical, present, satisfied, able to commit, feel emotions, still ego based... Liberated:- live fully, nothing is missing
- Famous 7s:- Jack Black, Oscar Wilde, Elizabeth Taylor, Miley Cyrus, Ted Danson, Elton John, Eddie Murphy, Robin Williams, Goldie Hawn, Lisa Kudrow

<u>Type 8:- The Challenger / The Leader / Protector</u>
- Confident, confrontational, strong personality, stand up for themselves and others, and decisive.
- Fear of being controlled, and struggle being vulnerable.
- They talk with their bodies, pulsating energy
- Even when listening, they are alert, dynamic.
- They are ready to be angry at any time if pushed and feel powerful and alive.
- Strong sense of self, capable, direct, just, not shy, tell it like it is. Right all wrongs.
- Push against limitations, turn blame outwards
- They are often short on patience, and what you see is what you get. They are very direct, work hard, and actions are often inspirational.
- They will stand up against bullies, and are honest and have great integrity.
- Work and career:- leaders, entrepreneurs, doctors, managers, police etc
- Continuum:- lower:- violent, rivals, ruthless... middle:- defiant, confrontational, grandiose, shrewd business people... Higher:- protective, leaders, strong, still ego based... Liberated:- surrendered innocence, know the source of real power.
- Famous 8s:- Jack Nicholson, Roseanne Barr, Danny Devito, Russel Crowe, Winston Churchill, Donald Trump, Kathy Bates

Type 9:- The peacekeeper / The Mediator

- Receptive, reassuring, agreeable, low key, avoid conflict. They seek peace and harmony, have a fear of loss.
- Avoid anger, want to please and go with the flow.
- They try and neutralise everything, so if people are down they try and bring them up, and if they are too high try and bring them down.
- They lack a sense of separate self, separate identity is too intense. They sometimes feel inferior.
- When they really don't want to do something, they will disappear, not respond to calls etc
- They avoid anger as it leaves them feeling limp and lacking energy
- The are positive, trusting, and tend to be optimistic in life. They want to create peace and can be naïve.
- They are sincere, and value relationships, and easy going most of the time.
- They are often called the salt of the earth and would help anyone.
- Work and career:- naturalists, landscapers, child educators, counsellors, anything related to healing
- Continuum:- lower:- dissociative, depressed... middle:- ignore problems, lost in routines, agree to things they don't want to do... Higher:- maintain peace, easy going, kind, dynamic, still ego based... Liberated:- loving acceptance, including difficult and uplifting experiences.
- Famous 9s:- Bill Clinton, Audrey Hepburn, Morgan Freeman, Abraham Lincoln, Queen Elizabeth II, Bill Murray, Santa Claus, Ronald Reagan.

They are the 9 Enneagram types at a basic level. It would be impossible to go much deeper in this book about the different variants such as the wings, subtypes, and going much deeper into the personalities of the types and strengths weaknesses etc.

If you want to go deeper into this fascinating subject I would suggest look into books focused solely on The Enneagram. It is a wonderful area, where you can go much deeper into people's personalities, and how to deal best with them in all situations.

We do go much deeper in the Enneagram in the 3 day 'Awakening Workshop' if you want to book on the 3 day workshop at www.thevikingbuddha.com

Chapter 22
The Key to your life

So let me ask you three questions...
1. Do you know who you are?
2. Do you know what you want?
3. Do you know why you are here?

If you can't answer all 3 of those questions, you are NOT living a fulfilled life!

Bruce Lee said "It is far greater a feat to conquer ONESELF than to conquer 10,000 more in battle"

Everybody is reaching for something they can't quite get... and this is because we don't know our answers.

We believe in physical laws, which we all live by, but unfortunately we leave it to luck, chance and coincidence in our personal lives.

So, what is the key to life? Most people want to accumulate, whether that be with money, houses, cars, possessions, status etc. Does all this make you truly happy?

The key to life is... love... you have to love life, you have to love what you do.

"Success without fulfilment is the ULTIMATE FAILURE"
Tony Robbins

You need to find yourself... become the master of yourself... you need to find your answers... conquer yourself...

The key to life is an acronym....
K-E-Y, Know Every You
So, a few more questions for you...
1. How is your life?
2. Are you enjoying it?
3. Are you happy?
4. Are you fulfilled?

5. Are you IN LOVE with life?

If the answers are no, why can't you create life you desire?

What is standing in your way? The simple answer is you! You are standing in your own way! You don't really know who you are!

When i say you don't know who you are, I am not talking about your name, race, your profession, religion, age, sex.. All those are your identity, your IDEA of who you are...

IDEA + ENTITY = IDENTITY

Your identity, is what is in the way of everything you really want in your life...

Your life should not be about fitting in, getting by, or trying to make it. You need to live your life ON PURPOSE...

Our environment creates our foundation of beliefs, and these foundations control everything we do, and everything that we are.

Do you know what the missing piece of the puzzle is for most of us? We have no idea who we are, and we have no idea what we really want, and we are totally in the dark as to why we are even here.

There always seems to be something missing, with those feelings of being incomplete, which leads us to search our lives to find things to fill this hole, we buy new things, find new relationships, but in the end, we are INCOMPLETE again.

When you do this, you are looking in the wrong direction... It's not out there, it is inside yourself!

If you feel broken, the reason is because you are NOT doing what you are supposed to be doing.

In life, we often find ourselves competing and comparing ourselves to other people for no reason, because you are not them, you are different from them, you are NOT supposed to be like anybody else.

You, are unique, you are individual, you have your own purpose in this world, we don't have to compete or compare ourselves with anyone else.

Your mind is creating everything in your world. Your mind is creating your life. Everything in the room that you are in, was created by a thought, Everything in the town or city that you live in, was created by a thought.

"Mind is everything, what you think you become, in a mind that is pure joy follows like a shadow that never leaves" Buddha

So, the question is are you in control of your own mind, and if the answer is yes, then why are creating the life you don't like or want?

You are not your mind... Your mind is your greatest tool...

It is a tool for you to use, for you to create the life that you want... it is your most valuable possession!

FACT... everything you have ever experienced was set into motion with your thoughts... If you react to the world negatively, you will experience negativity in all its forms...

If you react to the world positively, you will experience positivity in all its forms...

The universe is controlled by laws and systems, there is NO randomness. There is a law of thought, and it is CAUSE and EFFECT...

The mind is made up of one big story, made up from millions of little stories which is who you are. Your identity is just a story, everything you are, your life is just a story... Everything you have ever seen or sensed has a story attached to it.

We create our stories with our attention and our thoughts. Our thoughts tell us what to pay attention to, and we react to what we are paying attention to, which is our words and behaviour.

When you take away everything else, it is your true self which remains.... it is about your TRUE SELF... Our true self is ALWAYS there, even if you don't hear it. It is always communicating with us, with feelings and urges.

Have you ever woken up tired? Why does this happen? Because we are wasting all of our energy pretending to be someone we are not. We are not enthusiastic, we are not inspired about life.

When we are not living on purpose, we are literally killing ourselves. Ignoring your true self and pretending to be someone you are not, might just be KILLING YOU... So, what is it that makes you happy?

"Follow your bliss" Joseph Campbell

Become process orientated toward whatever it is you LOVE doing the most...And the rest will take care of itself!

"You know you have found your purpose when you start something at 6am and when you look up it is 10pm and you've forgotten to eat"
George Lucas

Every detail in our life is important, we need to become life Engineers! We need to find the faulty parts and structures,
Environment = construction site – culture – foundation
Our foundation should hold us up even when the ground is shaking.
The floor plan of our building is our needs, the walls and the ceiling are our values and rules, and our thoughts are the building blocks that build your entire life.
In order to change your life, you need to change the way that you think, you need to change your mind.
Neuroscientists say that our brain and body can't tell the difference between imagination and reality. We have 1 million sensory receptors in our brain that are built to deal with what we sense in our environment.
There are actually 10 billion receptors that are dedicated to imagination.
Physical senses do not create thought, thought actually creates physical senses.
There have been scientific studies with basketball players, where there was 10 basketball players, and they asked them to shoot free throws. 100 x free flows for 10 days. They took 10 other players, and got them to imagine shooting the same amount of free throws. The difference between the two outcomes when

they all went back on the court was the same. The imagination did the same amount of training for these people as the actual practice.

The key to health
You need to know every process that is happening inside your body. It is your health, nobody else's.

You need to take care of your body, if you want to live a happy and fulfilled life. The fact is that most of us have no conscious control over our health!

Why can't we control our body? Our beliefs are the reason why we are more often healthy or more often ill! We follow along and we become our environment. We believe what we are told to believe.

"The body is a world in itself, every little cell in your body is thinking, and communicating with the environment its surrounded by. Our emotions are chemical reactions to our thoughts"
Deepak Chopra

Pharmaceutical drugs are designed to mimic the chemicals that your body creates NATURALLY.

Whatever happens in the mind does not stay in the mind... it manifests in your body AND your life.

Key to your relationships
Our relationships are just as important as our health... in fact they often affect our health in many ways.

Relationships are about GIVING! It should be, how can I ADD to this person's life?

People coming together to make each other's lives BETTER.

Ask yourself this question... how are you fulfilling the 6 human needs of the people in your life? The certainty, the variety, contribution, love, significance, the growth...

When you master YOU... You will understand THEM...

FALL IN LOVE WITH LIFE... FALL IN LOVE WITH YOURSELF, cause that's when you can relate to the people in your life, because you can relate to them.
YOU MUST love YOU 1st...
Know yourself.... love yourself.... give yourself...

<u>The key to finances</u>
Money is an addiction for most people!
If money is just a tool for trading value, then how do you make more of it? RAISE YOUR VALUE!
There are only 2 reasons why you have not been able to accumulate more money...
1. You don't believe you have any more value to give.
2. Your values are conflicting.
You are in your OWN way... you need to raise your value to yourself, and to the world.
You have to find your purpose, and give that to the world, that will add value to others lives, and the more value you add to other people's lives, the more money you will make
When you chase your dream instead of the money, and go after your bliss, and find your purpose in life, the money starts chasing after you...

<u>The Key to life</u>
Paradise is a state of mind!
What you want, and what is missing in your life is also just a state of mind!
Your life is a reflection of your mind.

"Circumstances do NOT make the man, they reveal him to himself", *"You do NOT attract that which you want, but that which you are"* James Allen

Life is a GIFT.. Recognise your gift... Find your passion and what you love...

Chapter 23
Life Purpose Quest

So, let me ask you a question in the form of a scenario to start this chapter off. This is actually how I start off my motivational speeches and shows.

The question.... What if your life ended this minute?

Just imagine your life has suddenly ended, it happened this very second... no warning, no goodbyes, don't worry you felt nothing, it was just one of those things.

Take a moment for this to settle in.... your friends and family will be very upset, but no matter how loved you were, life WILL go on without you... how dare it right?

So... seeing you are dead, and you have an eternity on your hands... here are 3 important questions I want to ask you...

1. What did you love about your life?
2. Do you have any regrets now your life is over?
3. If you were given one more crack at living, what would you do?

I think you know what is coming next... you are about to get your life back, but before that happens... take a deep breath in, now exhale all the air from your lungs... and hold, and when you breathe back in again you are back alive...you have your life back...

SO, what will you do with the time you have been given?

Here are some questions to ask yourself... Be honest with yourself, and maybe this might be the start of the changes you have wanted in your life.

Discovering your passions and interests
- When you were a child, what did you want to be when you grew up?
- In the past as a child, what did you enjoy? Ie, food, activities, places visited, traditions you had, list what you liked and why.

- What are the current activities that bring you pleasure?
- What are the activities that you know you love, but may not be currently be doing, but would like to?
- What are the other aspects of your life that bring you joy, excitement and that energise you?
- What are you truly passionate about?
- What are your best qualities?
- When are you most yourself?
- What makes you feel in the flow?
- What comes easy to you that may be hard for others?
- YOUR DREAMS... what do YOU really want?
- If you could have anything you want, what would it be?
- Your values... what do you stand for?
- What would you change in the world?
- In what way can YOU be the change in the world?
- What are the aspects in your life you are committed to
- What are the dreams, gifts, and passions you are committed to fulfilling in your life?
- What would it take for you to be living in integrity?

Here is an exercise for you to do, and it is called Your life story:-

- The past:- write a story of your past. Be sure to describe the main lessons you have learned, the challenges you have overcome, and the personal strengths you have developed along the way.
- The present:- write a description of where you are in your life today. Write about what is good in your life. Who you are to other people, what you have, who you are about, and what you are grateful for
- The future:- what do you see in your future? What are you excited about in your future? And who are you willing to become for other people? How can you become more grounded within yourself?

In my motivational workshops I do these next 2 examples as demonstrations. The first one is called 4 Important lessons for a simple life.
- Get a pencil with an eraser on the end of it. There are 4 things you need to know before you go out on the world and be the person you want to be. Remember these things, and you will be the best person you can be.
- 1st:- look at the pencil. We know that in order for it to become a useful pencil, that from time to time, again and again, it is going to have to go through re-sharpening, and if this pencil could feel, we can only imagine how painful that would be, but that is what it takes, for it to be a useful pencil. Life is much the same, painful experiences and challenges come to us all, but it is through these opportunities that we build character, and we grow.
- 2nd:- is to keep in mind that we will be able to correct many of the mistakes along the way just like the eraser. We learn from our mistakes, they are not mistakes, they are lessons we can use to do better the next time round.
- 3rd:- just like the pencil, every place where you, are you, so to speak, you leave your mark. You are writing your own story, think of the stumbling blocks as stepping stones and NEVER stop writing.
- 4th:- always remember, the most important part of the pencil is what is inside.

You can be anything you want to be in your life, You just need to have the belief in yourself, and go and live the life you were meant to live.

The next story i tell in my workshops and motivational speeches, is again one about never giving up, and realising that the only thing that is holding you back, is YOU.

<u>What elephants can teach us about human freedom</u>

There was once a man who passed by a travelling circus one day. When he saw a few of the elephants, he stopped suddenly, he was curious, and confused.

How is it that these big creatures were standing there with just one small rope around one front leg, not trying to break away?

There were no cages, no chains, and yet they are big enough so obviously they can get away any time they wanted to.

He saw the trainer nearby, and he wanted to ask the trainer, how is it that they have a little rope around their leg and they were not even trying to break away

The trainer said, "well, when they are much younger, we used to use the same size rope on them, and then it was easy to hold them. They became conditioned to believe after a while that they could never break away"

Well like the elephants, many of us go through life holding onto the belief that we can't do something simply because we failed at it once before.

So what, you fail once, maybe twice, maybe 100 times, but like Edison said, "I've not failed, I have just found 10,000 ways that don't work. Failure is a part of learning, you should never give up and struggle in life, Find your dream and your purpose in life. So again, ask yourself these questions below...

Benefits to yourself
- What are your TRUE desires?
- What areas in your life are in need of the most transformation.
- What are the most important roles that you need to change in order to be living in authenticity?
- What are you MOST Passionate about?
- What do you believe to be your life's mission - your greatest purpose?
- Who is your favourite role model? In what ways do you identify yourself in this person?
- How do you feel about your ability to change both the circumstances of your life and your behaviours and skills as well?
- What triggers or habits have you determined you would like to change? What are your plans for changing them?
- What strategies do you have in place for practicing uncertainty to become more accustomed to the uncertainty of life change?

Any goals you come up in your life have to be SMART Specific, Measurable, Achievable, Realistic and Time framed. So, what goals can you set yourself to get the life you want?

Below is a Life Purpose Questionnaire. It is time to look at what really makes you tick, and what you love to do most, before we take things a step further in the next chapter.

Life Purpose Questionnaire
- Make a list of the roles you play in your life
- Rate your current life on a scale from 1-100, with 100 being the best possible life.
- Now list the positive realities in your life.
- Now list the negative possibilities in your life.
- Create a snapshot in your mind of your ideal life.
- What do you LOVE to do?
- What would you do for free?
- What do you love to learn and talk about?
- What would you regret never trying?
- If someone were able to look in your private library, what would they find?
- What SPARKS your creativity?
- What activities, hobbies, projects, or people make you smile?
- Looking back at your life, what were your favourite things to do? What about now?
- What activities make you lose track of time?
- What makes you feel great about yourself?
- Who inspires you the most? This could be people you know or don't know. Which qualities inspire you in each person?
- What skills, abilities, or gifts are you naturally good at?
- What do people typically ask you for help in?
- If you had to teach something, what would you teach?
- What would you regret not fully doing, being or having in your life?

One day a dad was cooking in the kitchen, when his daughter walked into the kitchen with something on her mind. The dad said what's wrong?

His daughter said, "school is so hard, the content is impossible, and I don't think I will ever make it to 4th grade"

Her dad smiled, and took out 3 pots, he filled them with water and put them on the hob. The 3 pots began to boil. He placed a potato into the 1st pot, eggs into the 2nd pot, and coffee beans into the 3rd pot. The daughter asked what he was doing, and he said patience sweetheart.

After 20 minutes he took the potatoes out of the pot, and placed them on a plate. He did the same with the eggs, and then he poured the coffee into a mug. He then said to his daughter "what do you see?"

He then said look closer… the potatoes, the eggs, and the coffee beans, each faced the same adversity in boiling water, however, each one of them reacted differently.

The potato went in strong and unrelenting, but in the boiling water, it became soft and weak. The egg was fragile, with the thin outer shell protecting its liquid interior, until it was placed in the boiling water, then it became hard.

However, the coffee beans were unique, after they were exposed to the hot boiling water, they changed it and created something new… which are you? He asked his daughter.

When adversity knocks on your door, how do you respond? Are you a potato? The egg or coffee bean?

In life things happen around us, things happen to us, but what truly matters is what happens within us.

Which one are you?

To finish this chapter off, I am going to give you another scenario to visualise and imagine

- You are now 90 years old, sitting in your rocking chair outside. You can feel the spring breeze gently brushing against your face.
- You are blissful and happy, and are pleased with the wonderful life you have been blessed with.

- Looking back at your life, and all that you have achieved and acquired, and all the relationships you have developed.
- What matters the most?

You are never too late to get the life you dream about and desire. The key is to find out what you are passionate about and love doing, and take that chance to make it happen. Don't regret not doing things later on in life. If you are passionate about something and want to do it for a living, it will come true and you will get your dream job, and life you want.

Chapter 24
Your Ikigai

So, what is Ikigai?

The word Ikigai is Japanese for your reason for being. It is also the reason you get out of bed in the morning. Your sense of purpose, the things you live for, the things that make your life worthwhile, and your springboard for tomorrow.

Your ikigai is personal to you and your life, which goes in line with your values and beliefs.

Ikigai can help you to find peace within yourself and also with the world, live a life that is authentically YOU, be more of the things that bring you joy and also help you find out what is REALLY important to you.

"There are many ways to define Ikigai, Ikigai is a spectrum, The complexity of Ikigai, actually reflects the complexity of life itself" Ken Mogi

The Ikigai framework is basically 4 circles which includes what you love, what you are good at, what the world needs, and what you can be rewarded for.

So let me ask you 3 more questions...

1. Are your thought patterns and mindsets holding you back or moving you forward?

2. How are you approaching your daily life and tasks and interactions with others?

3. How are you structuring your days and spending your time?

Ikigai is about living a balanced lifestyle which includes your goals, actions, rituals, thoughts, attitudes, habits, time and energy.

There are 5 pillars of Ikigai
1. Start small:- focus on the details.
2. Release yourself:- accept who you are.
3. Harmony and sustainability:- rely on others
4. The joy of the little things:- appreciate sensory pleasure
5. Be in the here and now:-find your flow.

The first Pillar:- when you are starting small, pay attention to things that excite you and interest you, and give them a chance for them to grow into something bigger.

The second Pillar:- When you are releasing yourself, you need to tune into the present moment, accept yourself for who you are, understand the things that are not in your control, and let go of singular ideas of happiness.

A man said to buddha, "I want happiness" Lond buddha said "first remove the "I" that's ego, then remove the "want", that's desire, what are you left with? "happiness"

The third Pillar:- With harmony and sustainability, it is good to be able to self-reflect. Ask yourself these questions.
- What have I received from others?
- What have I given to others?
- What troubles have I caused others?

Understand how your decisions AND your indecisions impact on others. We need to mindful on how our decisions affect others.

The 4th pillar of Ikigai is the joy of the little things.

"Ikigai isn't a grand target, it is a spectrum of small things. The really big things might only happen once a decade, so life isn't sustainable without the small daily joys" Ken Mogi

The little things could be taking time out for yourself, sunbathing, spending time with loved ones, your morning cup of coffee, disconnecting from your phone, or discovering a new place or city.

The fifth Pillar of Ikigai is to FIND YOUR FLOW...

This means being in the here and now... you need to find your flow. This is all about presence and intention. Being in the moment and locked in the process...

It is about channelling your focus and concentration into a task or activity, and enjoying experience.

Finding your flow includes doing some of the following
- Reducing worries and concerns
- Increasing your focus.
- Enhancing positive feelings like self-acceptance and self-confidence
- Sharpening your problem solving and decision making, And increasing your productivity and creativity.

You need to get rid of distractions, avoid multitasking, choose tasks that you enjoy, don't overthink things, and keep practicing.

There are 10 rules of Ikigai, and here they are...

1. Stay active, don't retire.

2. Take it slow. When you leave urgency behind life takes on a new meaning. Don't rush anything.

3. Don't fill your stomach. Less is more when it comes to a long life. Eat a little less than your hunger demands.

4. Surround yourself with good friends. We are social beings, so we need good friendships for positivity, support and guidance.

5. Get in shape for your next birthday. It isn't about exercising the most, it is about moving the most., i.e, gardening, swimming, hiking, dancing, yoga,

6. Smile. Think of each day as a new day with the opportunity to make yourself happy and others happy around you.

7. Reconnect with nature. Spending time in nature helps us get back in touch with ourselves, and the benefits are incredible for your wellbeing. It has a grounding affect, and is excellent for our spiritual and physical health.

8. Give thanks. Be thankful for your life, and the things in your life every day.

9. Live in the moment. Be present and give yourself fully to everything you do.

10. Find your Ikigai. Find your passion. Your mission is to discover YOUR Ikigai.

Ikigai is a way of life, a state of mind, having life goals, and the small joys in life, and having an abstract vision.

Your Ikigai is about your passions, strengths, opportunities, and contributions which can be further broken down into your core values, achievements, hobbies and interests, skills and talents, your career, opportunities to grow, your impact, and legacy, relationships, your vision for the world, your hope for the future, and your extrinsic and intrinsic motivations.

So, this is where we revisit what you love...

- What brings you the most happiness
- What were the things you loved to do as a child?
- What are the things you love to do now?
- What are the roles and relationships that bring out the best in you?

And here is a good question... how would you spend your time if you were only given 1 year to live?

What are you good at? What are your skills, expertise, and where you have most knowledge?

What makes you unique? What are your best personality traits? What are the things that come naturally to you?

Another area to think about is what the world needs, and what you can bring to others and the world.

What can you do for others? What are your hopes for the future? What social issues are important to you? Whose life accomplishments inspire you to be a better person? How can you put your skills to use in support of others?

What you really need to do is:-

- Identify what you want to do more of, and do less of, and what areas you want to continue to work on.
- Make time for the things that bring you happiness and fulfilment.
- Focus your time and energy on the things that matter the most.

- Create the life that you want to live, cultivate good habits, and do more of what you love. Continue to get to know yourself, and focus on life-long growth and development.

Wabi Sabi
Wabi:- Rusticness, isolation or simplicity
Sabi:- beauty that comes with age and withering

Life is impermanent, tomorrow is never guaranteed, so don't take anything for granted, and act now on the things that you want to do.

Life is imperfect, and no matter how much we plan, we can't control everything, the more we accept that life in imperfect, the better we are able to respond when bad things happen.

The one thing we can control is our response.

Life is incomplete. We are a work in progress, and it is about the process and not the end result, so take steps forward at your OWN pace.

Kintsugi
Resilience, self-care and self-love
Kintsugi is the art of repairing broken items with gold.

Self-love:- our struggles, flaws, pains and imperfections are an integral part of who we are. Kintsugi teaches us to embrace our imperfections so we can find a greater sense of appreciation for ourselves.

Self-care:- all of life's challenges and pain can be healed, but it takes time, patience, and effort to turn your cracks into GOLD.

No matter how many times you fall or break, you can always pick up the pieces and continue to shine.

There is another practical demonstration which i do in the workshops and motivational speeches and it is called the £20 note. And it goes something like this.

The £20 Note
I get a £20 our and ask the following questions
- Who would like this £20, and of course everyone says "I do" I then proceed to crumple it up, and ask the same question again.

- Who wants the £20 note now? And of course everyone still wants the £20. So now I put it on the floor, and step all over it.. And ask the same question, and of course everyone still wants it...

The important lesson is that no matter what I did with the £20, they still wanted it because it never lost its worth. There are many times in our lives, when we feel like life has crumpled us up and ground us into the dirt.

We make some bad decisions or have to deal with some poor circumstances, and sometimes life can make us feel worthless, but no matter what happens, no matter what will happen, you never lose your worth, you never lose your value, DON'T EVER FORGET THAT.

So, in much the same way, that the bowl in Kintsugi can be repaired, and is still valuable, no matter what you go through in life, you are still worth it, and can change everything and grow.

No matter how many times you fall or break, you can always pick up the pieces and continue to shine.

Kaizen

You may have heard of Kaizen, and this is about continuous improvement.

"Ikigai is the action we take in pursuit of happiness"
Yukari Mitsuhashi

So, Kaizen is the practice of continuous improvement or change for the better. 1% improvement each day.

With patience and commitment to small, incremental, and daily actions, you can create new habits, and make big changes in your life.

The 8 areas of wellness

1. Physical:- we need to recognise the need for physical activity, diet, nutrition and enough sleep to take care of our bodies.
2. Intellectual:- we need to explore our creative abilities, and find ways to expand our knowledge and experiences.
3. Emotional:- we need to understand and care for ourselves so we are able to cope and find joy in our lives.

4. Environmental:- we need to care for our environment, connect with nature, and live in places that support our well-being.

5. Spiritual:- we need to find inner peace, harmony, sense of purpose and our meaning in life.

6. Financial:- reaching a sense of satisfaction with our finances is something we should do, so we can live comfortably within our means.

7. Social:- as human beings, as social beings, we need to create healthy relationships with others, and develop conenctions with others

8. Occupational:-we need to find satisfaction, and our purpose, where we find enrichment and feel sense of contribution

The most important thing to take away from this chapter is to build long lasting and life changing habits. Aim for 1% improvement every day. Stay accountable to yourself, give yourself the flexibility to build up or scale down, focus on one or two goals, and give your full attention and energy to those goals.

Hansei
This is the art of self-reflection
"*You can't connect the dots looking forward, you can only connect them looking backward*" Steve Jobs

Han:- to change, turn over, or turn upside down
Sei:- to look back upon, review or examine oneself.
Take personal responsibility and accountability for your actions, and take a good look at your flaws, weaknesses, and growth opportunities and strengths.

What makes a great leader?
Another practical demonstration I do in the workshops is to ask the attendees what makes a great leader? And I then say "In this box I have a picture of one of the world's greatest leaders over the last 100 years, and I ask them to guess who it is in the box.

And of course, I get many different answers from Winston Churchill, to Nelson Mandela, and many other names. Then I ask "what qualities make for a good leader?" ... then I Hand the box over to different people for them to look inside the box and see who it actually is... what do you think they see in that box?

They see themselves!! It is a mirror in the box.. what can we learn from this?

We are all leaders, we can become leaders. If we tap into our full potential, we can be anything we want to be.

There is only one person that can prevent you from being the best that you can be, and that person is YOU! You are the only one, who can revolutionize YOUR life. You are the only one who can influence your happiness, and your success.

Your life doesn't change when your boss changes, or when your career changes, your life changes when YOU change.

When you get beyond your limited beliefs, when you realise that YOU are the only one who is responsible for your life, then you can be whoever and whatever you want to be. Allow yourself to be the best you can be. The world needs great leaders, now more than ever, its time to believe in YOURSELF.

Part 3
The Awakening

Chapter 25
Universal Law

<u>The 10 Spiritual Laws</u>
1. We are all pure consciousness:- we are pure energy beings, and we will always be in existence. We are indestructible. We have come onto this earth to have a human experience. After the experience we will pass on and move into another body. Imagine that we are in a theme park, and we are always returning back for another ride until you complete all the rides. We all have a return ticket forever, and part of coming down and having the human experience, we all have our own agendas, the things we need to experience in this life on earth. The people that we interact in this life are in our soul groups, and they are the souls we have agreed to come down and play out our experiences with.
2. All is one:- every single thing in the universe is interconnected, and everything is made of the same structure, which is pure energy, it just has different vibrations.
3. There is only now:- everything exists now, there is no past or future. There is only now, the present.
4. The law of attraction:- whatever you put out to the universe, you will get back, If you think negative things and thoughts, that is what you will get back, If you think positive that is what you will get back.
5. Everything in existence is subject to change, except for 1,2,3,4. People don't like change, but you should embrace change, look forward to change.

6. In every moment, and from moment to moment, you are a different person. You change every single moment. Your cells are renewing all the time. Every single second you are a different person. Every single second you are reset perfect, you are reborn. This is until you pay attention to something else, and we go back, and still live the same lives with the same problems, because you don't change your cells, and your thinking, and your mindset to make those changes, and make the universe work for you.

7. Reality is meaningless:- Reality is waiting for you to give it your meaning. The reality comes from whatever meaning you give to it. Your reality can only have 3 options, a positive, neutral or negative meaning. There are actually billions of possibilities, but they all come down to just 3. Positive, negative or neutral.

8. Respect others:- allow them to be right. They are on a different journey to yours, they have a different plan and agenda to yours, and it is not for you to judge them. Respect their journey and their life.

9. Gratitude:- Always be grateful. For everything in your life be grateful. Be grateful for the people around you, your house, your family. Thank the universe for everything which is good in life, and also for every situation good or bad.

10. Live for every moment. From moment to moment, live in that moment. Do the things that you love and what makes you happy. Do the things you are passionate about. Don't have expectations, they only cause pain, just live in the moment.

Universal Laws

There are 12 Universal Laws, and they are all interconnected, just as we are all interconnected.

1. Law of Divine Oneness:- All the things, the people around you are all connected. We are all one. Everything in the universe is interconnected. Every action, thought, event, is connected to everything else.

2. Law of Vibration:- Everything on the earth, everything in the universe, is in constant motion. Everything is energy, and everything is vibrating at specific frequencies. We are all energy, and we have a specific vibration. Trees, buildings, cars, are all

energy vibrating at different frequencies. All our thought, feelings, words have different vibrational frequencies.

3. Law of correspondence:- the Phrase 'as above, so below, as within, so without' relates to the law of correspondence, as whatever is happening inside of us, our thoughts, worries, actions, is what makes our reality outside. Our reality outside mirrors our thoughts, feelings, and what we are asking the universe for on the inside.

4. The Law of Attraction:- This law we discuss in the next chapter, and this is used for manifesting what you want from the universe. Like attracts like, so if your feelings are negative, and you have money worries, and doubt, and negative feelings about yourself, then the universe will provide more of that for you. But if your thoughts are positive, and you ask the universe for all the positive things you want in life, then the universe will provide you with those things in due course. You get what you focus on, but also you need to believe what you are wanting is possible to obtain. You need to see yourself having these things and this positive future. You need to keep your vibrational frequency high.

5. Law of Inspired Action:- this law basically means you need to be proactive, and take those real steps towards the things that you want in your life. You need to be open to all possibilities, take action to get the things you desire in your life.

6. Law of perpetual Transmutation of Energy:- Everything in the universe is constantly changing and evolving. Every thought produces an action, and these thoughts eventually have the power to manifest into our reality. So you need to learn to keep those thoughts positive, and change any negatives to positives. When you are near someone who is negative, and has low energy, you normally feel yourself becoming depleted, unless you get away from them, whilst at the same time, being around someone who is upbeat and positive, it starts to rub off on you and raises your vibration. You need to keep your vibration and frequency high. Maintain positive feelings, thoughts and actions.

7. Law of Cause and Effect:- Every action has a reaction. If you feel angry or sad or upset, you are putting out that energy to the universe, and it will come back to you at some point. If you put out good vibrations to the universe, it will come back to you as those positive energies and thoughts and actions at some point.

8. Law of Compensation:- The old saying 'you reap what you sow' is true with the Law of Compensation. Whatever you put in you will get out, or whatever you put out the universe you will get back. Your positive efforts will always come back with positivity from the universe. If you are angry and nasty with people around, you will get that right back at you. If you are kind, loving, empathetic, caring with everyone around you, you will get that back from the universe.

9. Law of Relativity:- Everything is neutral, the law of relativity exists in all things and everything around us. In the end the meaning comes down to our perspective and our perception. Appreciate everything you have, don't compare with others.

10. Law of Polarity:- The law of polarity is basically saying everything In life has an opposite, love-fear, warm-cold, good-evil. If you are going through a rough time at the moment, grab hold of that coin, and try and flip it over and see if you can get a new perspective, and a way to go forward with that new side of the coin. Always try and find the positives in life.

11. Law of Rhythm:- Nothing is permanent. The universe has cycles, just as the earth does, and just as we do. We cannot be the same all the time, but we are changing all the time, and we go through stages, good and bad, but none of them are permanent. Nothing is permanent.

12. Law of Gender:- There is masculine and feminine energy in all that is around us, what you need to learn to do is find your own balance between the divine masculine, and divine feminine.

There are 21 universal sub-laws and they are:-
• Aspiration, CHARITY, COMPASSION, courage, Dedication, faith, FORGIVENESS, GENEROSITY, grace, HONESTY, hope, joy, KINDNESS, leadership, noninterference, PATIENCE, PRAISE, responsibility, SELF-LOVE, THANKFULNESS, UNCONDITIONAL LOVE.

I have highlighted some of the 21 sub-laws, as it just shows it is really important to give yourself some self-love, and show everyone around you love, forgiveness, kindness, compassion, will all give positive vibrations out to the universe, and remember, we are all on a different mission in our lives, with different agendas, and different problems, so always be kind.

Chapter 26
The Law of Attraction

Whether you know it or not, every day you are reciting affirmations that program your mind and your life.

The positive affirmations such as I am healthy, I am wealthy, I am awesome, can work wonders for you and also in your life.

Unfortunately, the negative affirmations such as I am stupid, I am broke, I am fat, I am so tired, have a very negative effect on our lives.

"B*e mindful of your self-talk because it's a conversation with the universe"* David James Lees

We are, and attract into our lives, what we say, think and believe about ourselves and our perceived reality.

Have you ever felt like you were going crazy at any time, because things just weren't working out the way you wanted them too? The chances are you have been wanting something different from your statements, yet your life really is from the results of the things that you have programmed into it.

You can make the change! You can make the change to be positive...the change to a happier, healthier and more abundant life.

Albert Einstein defined insanity as, "doing the same thing over, and over again, and expecting different results"

Two of the most powerful words which can shape your reality are... I AM... Depending what you put after those words.

"I AM" means that I am one with the creative power of God

"I AM" means that I am one with the creative power of life

"I AM" means that I am one with the creative power of the universe.

When you say "I AM", and concentrate on positive things, you create positive experiences in your life.

"Whether you think you can, or you think that you can't, You're absolutely right" Henry Ford

If you believe you are sick, unworthy and destined to fail... You are!

Look beyond your present fears, negativity and pain, and create positive results in your life.

Change your way of thinking, and realise that you control your emotions, and don't allow your emotions to control you.

You cannot speak in negative terms about your future, yourself and your life, and then expect positive results.

Remember... "we are, and attract into our lives, what we think, say and believe about ourselves and our perceived reality"

When you say things like "I am so stupid, "I am so fat and ugly", you are affirming this as your reality, and you will feel stupid, fat and ugly.

You have got to send your words out in the direction you want your life to go. If you want to know what you will be like five years from now, just listen to what you are saying about yourself now.

The most important factor is to BELIEVE. When you ask for something and don't believe that you can have it, it does not manifest, because your vibration does NOT match to your desire.

A positive mental attitude is the key to our success and happiness in life. The realisation is imperative, and once you truly comprehend this, it truly is life-changing. The steps of this attraction are really simple.

ASK - BELIEVE – RECEIVE

The law of attraction is constant, and always at work in your life.

Most people think that the Law of Attraction occurs on a subconscious level... NOT TRUE... it is at work in every thought you have, every word you speak, and every emotion.

Every one of your thoughts has a frequency. Our thoughts generate specific frequencies, or vibrations of energy and send them into the universe. The universe returns events and experiences into our lives that support our beliefs and correspond with our emotional frequency.

When you are overwhelmed with frustrating situations causing never ending problems and anxiety in your life, you will continue to attract these catastrophic episodes that keep provoking these feelings and circumstances.

When things are really going well, and you are experiencing good events and situations, and when you are experiencing pleasure in your life, you will keep attracting more positive and blissful situations,

Here's a question, how many times have you said, yeah it's great now, but I am just waiting for something to go wrong? So, you successfully manifest a great situation in your life, then attract the loss of that situation, because you bring negative into it.

You get to choose what follow your "I AM", and what you want to attract in your life. It really is that simple. You, and your life will be as good as your thoughts and spoken affirmations.

You must change any, and all negative thought patterns to positive thoughts and emotions about yourself and your reality.

If you believe you can never get ahead financially, you only deserve just enough money to barely get by, or there's never enough, your subconscious will emit these thought frequencies to the universe, and you will attract back into your life these exact situations to support your perceived reality.

If you stress about your bills, fight with your spouse about money, and worry about how you are going to make the next payment, that is the exact signal or frequency you are broadcasting to the universe.

Obsessing over your financial problems, only makes matters worse. The more you stress the worse it gets, because you keep attracting more negativity back into your reality.

The more you focus on doubt, jealousy, frustration, fear, stress, judgement, and worry, the more you are calling these negative emotions into your life.

We have all had our struggles in life, but it doesn't matter what has happened in your past, it is your choice to move forward and reprogram your subconscious to rid yourself of thoughts and behaviours of low self-worth.

What we believe, we manifest into our lives. So, change your thinking, and change your life. Believe in yourself!

Remember like attracts like... we, are that which we think about most...you must train yourself to constantly be, and stay happy to receive this higher level of being.

Your subconscious mind doesn't know when you are joking, it simply follows orders. Once your conscious mind believes and accepts something as a true desire, the information is transferred to your subconscious mind.

If you say, "every winter I get the flu", your subconscious creates and manifests the flu for you.

The good thing about the subconscious/conscious mind, is that it is controlled by YOU.

You decide what to believe, what to desire, and what orders to give your subconscious mind.

You can bring great abundance to your life, and get the life you desire, by believing, and also saying positive affirmations, and remember I AM is so powerful.

- I AM creating my life
- The law of attraction is giving me positive favour.
- I AM, and i attract whatever I think, say and believe.
- I AM always prepared
- I AM worthy
- I AM sustaining true happiness
- I AM living the life I desire
- I AM affirming my desires
- I AM always grateful
- I AM healthy, wealthy and happy.
- I AM Succesful

Vision boards are another way to effectively program your subconscious mind. Your vision boards should have photos, images, and positive affirmations on it, and you should also make sure your vision boards are visible, and you look at it often. On your vision board you should also write and affirm, "I am always blessed with more than enough money to get anything I truly desire" it doesn't have to be money, but it is the positive affirmation, and you being able to see that regularly on your vision board.

Affirmations are very powerful for manifesting what you desire from the universe, because every time you read or listen to an affirmation it becomes a stronger force in your life.

"By repeating an affirmation over, and over again it becomes embedded in the subconscious mind and eventually becomes your reality" Tony Robbins

What you need to do with your positive affirmations is you should recite them several times a day.

So, let's go a little deeper into the Law of Attraction and how to master it.

Always remember to keep your thoughts and actions positive. If you think and feel more of illness and disease, than health, they guess what, illness and disease is what will manifest.

Remember cause and effect... your vibration is cause, and manifestation is effect. What you think and feel the most, will ultimately manifest in your life.

The law of attraction doesn't care who you are, where you are, where you come from or what you look like.

The Law of Attraction only cares about what you feel the most, where you turn your attention to the most, and what you talk about the most...

Vibration is cause... Manifestation is effect.

Nothing ever comes into your experience uninvited, it comes because you want it, or because you don't want it. Whatever manifests in your life does so because you have been in vibrational alignment with it. Where there is vibrational alignment, manifestation must occur, at some point, in due time.

This means, whatever you manifest, won't happen overnight, just like a seed planted in the soil, it needs time to grow, so does manifestation.

You are a vibrational being, every single thought you think, and every feeling that you feel emits an energetic vibration. When you have feelings of worry, doubt, fear they emit low vibrational frequencies, and things like joy and gratitude give off high vibration frequencies. It is not really the thought that evokes the sacred laws but more what you feel.

Nothing is attracted into your life, as much as it actually emerges from within you, via what you are in vibrational harmony with. What you are experiencing in this moment, is simply what you have brought into your life with what you have previously thought and felt. So, what you predominantly think and feel today, will manifest in a future moment.

So, now do you see why you need to positive, grateful, and always give out positive vibrations.

Nobody and nothing can make you think anything, unless you give them the power to do so. If you want to master the Law of Attraction, you need to take your mind back and begin to think for yourself.

If you want to be healthy, you first need to feel more healthy, regardless of your present health. If you want more money, you first need to feel more abundance, regardless of your present finances. You need to keep your high vibrational frequencies regardless of your current circumstances.

When 51% or more of your thoughts and feelings are more aligned with what you want, than what you don't want, then that is when manifestation of what you really do want and desire begins to gain momentum.

Whatever you are going through in your life, you need to find a way to think more about what you want, and positive vibrations, than what you don't want.

You need to know what you want... you need to want it enough, like a burning desire. Desire and attention are the two most powerful creative agents there are. You need to think, feel and act in alignment with what you desire.

So, question time... what do you want?... Who do you want to be?... what do you want to do?

You need to take the lid off the jar of your limitations, and catch YOUR life's highest vision. Allow yourself to tune into your heart's desire.

The thing is, you don't need to know how your dream will manifest, or even when it will manifest. You job is to have a big dream for your life, and believe in the process.

Gratitude plays a big part in the Law of Attraction, and realising and acknowledging all the good that is present in your life, because where there is gratitude there can be no fear, worry or doubt.

The more you turn your attention towards what you do want, the more of that will flow into your life.

The Key.... be grateful for anything.... be Grateful for everything.

When you have your vision, if you do not move towards your vision, you will NOT evoke the law of attraction to work for you. Most people don't act upon their dreams and desires... and guess what, they remain merely dreamers.

Through your thoughts and feelings, you set something in motion, and through your actions you allow that something to come into manifestation.

DO SOMETHING EVERY SINGLE DAY... that moves you closer to manifesting what you desire. While you are doing it, take on the feeling tone that it is already being done.

When you feel inspired to do something... do it. You may be challenged to go outside your current comfort zone, you will be called to grow. You may experience doubt, worry and fear, but choose to trust LIFE more than fear.

The only thing that is standing between your dream and you, are you own limited thoughts, opinions, perceptions and judgements. If you want your vision and dreams to manifest, you need to move through the fear.

KEEP DOING SOMETHING EVERY SINGLE DAY... big or small it doesn't matter, just do it.

Choose to hang out with those who...
- Inspire you
- Empower you
- Support you

No matter how far you have come, you are simply just getting started. Each moment is a new beginning, that offers the possibility to go even wider, deeper and higher, and beyond your dreams, and maybe something even bigger, greater and grander awaits....

Remember... YOU, and only YOU, are responsible for YOU...

Nobody and nothing can make you think or feel anything, unless YOU give them that power.

YOU get to choose what you feel and think in any given moment.

And choose to give energy, only to that which serves YOU

Chapter 27
Reality Transmuting

Reality transmuting is a practical method which is based on the Universal laws, that can teach you on how to move towards the space of variations to manifest your ideal life.

Reality Transmuting is based on the newest discoveries of quantum physics, and it also based on Universal laws also.

You are really special, because you are part of the creation, you are part of the universe.

You need to change your inner coding, which is in your conscious and subconscious mind. To change your outer world, you need to change your inner world. Your negative beliefs, thoughts and how you view the world need to be re-coded, so you can change your outer world, and manifest all the things you have been afraid to do in your life, because of what your current beliefs and restrictions inside you are stopping you from achieving.

The key to everything is energy! You have infinite possibilities! You have infinite lines of possibility in the universe

Everything that you wish for, everything that you want, already exists, it just doesn't exist in this dimension, but it does exist. All the possible realities are existing as kind of like a film /movie, and you already have the whole film projected, you have the past moments, the present moments and future moments.

Remember time does not exist, it is an illusion of the 3rd dimension. All our timelines are co-existing, they are all happening right now. This is why it is so important to live in the present moment.

Due to energy we can move towards the space of variations and manifesting different realities for ourselves. Every single thing in the universe is energy, and everything has a frequency. We are connected to other people around the world, animals, plants, trees, the universe, because we are part of the quantum field.

The reality you are experiencing right now, is only one of the infinite possibilities available to you. Whatever you want in your life, whatever you want to manifest in your life, already exists, but it is simply expressed in another line of reality, but you can that line of reality through energy.

The intention you give out to the universe must be:-

- Short:- you need to learn to be articulate, and for your intention to be short, and to the point.
- Clear:- You need to be clear in what your mind as to what you want to manifest.
- Strong;- This means you need to focus, and put all of your energy, and desire into your intention. You need to feel it, perceive it, mean it.
- Detachment:-You need to let go of the intention, and have confidence in the universe to provide this for us. Once you have set your intention and manifested it to the universe, allow the universe work for you.

What you need to start being aware of is the level of your energy. Your thoughts trigger emotions, and your thoughts have energy and different frequencies. Positive emotions have good frequencies, and a positive outcome on the energy in your body.

Your thoughts and emotions and their vibrations are the reason why you are in your current reality, good or bad.

You need to make sure you take care of your physical body, and stay healthy. We are made up of 70% water, so it is so important to drink water. All the food and drink you have, alcohol etc, have energy and frequencies too, and you need to make sure you keep your body in good shape and eat the things with keep your frequency at a high level.

You also need to make sure you surround yourself with people with high frequency levels and good energy, or they can take your energy and frequency levels, and this affects you manifesting the life you want.

You need to learn to not overreact, and respond negatively to situations, as it affects your emotions. If you are feeling negative energies and emotions internally, this will affect your frequency and vibration, and will affect your outer world. You need to try and keep your reactions balanced.

So what are they key principles of Reality Transmuting?
1. Keep it simple. Keep it real and true. Enjoy the small things and you will be manifest great things.
2. The evolution of your own consciousness. It is important to raise your vibrations and frequencies and raise your spiritual awareness and go through evolution for your spirit and soul
3. Stay true. Stay true to your heart, mind, soul. Stay true to yourself.

As you develop these skills, you will find that your spiritual consciousness will start ascending to an higher level.

What you need to get rid of is your old conditionings, your old beliefs, certain values, beliefs from peers and society, from our families and parents, who managed to give a lot of negative conditioning, beliefs and trauma.

Once you can get rid of your ego and your conditioning, you can raise your spiritual awareness, your energy and your frequency,. You can ascend to a higher level of energy and towards spiritual enlightenment.

So why do we always manifest our biggest fears?

Because as the saying goes 'the energy flows where the attention goes', and if we are always focusing on our biggest fears, that is what we are going to manifest and attract. These feelings are really intense, and all your thoughts and emotions will manifest more fears and negative reality.

Unfortunately, we are all part of the system, 'the matrix' which is the conditioning our parents, grandparents, and other peers were brainwashed to follow.

This becomes our reality, the beliefs, what we are told, and the conditioning from our peers and family, and parents, schools etc, and this is why many people are unable to get what they truly desire, because they are stuck in this matrix.

From the moment we are born until now, we are conditioned by other people's beliefs, society, the people in power, media, and we are pretty much told we can't go out and get what we truly desire, and in many ways we are told by our parents who were told by their parents, that we can't have what all these other people who have fancy cars, houses and wonderful lives, and this is wrong, it is false.

But to get what you truly desire and want out of your life, and live your perfect life, you need to break free of your conditionings, and the matrix.

If you want to get the life you want and get the universe to manifest the life that is waiting there for you if you truly desire it, stop listening to the news, the newspapers, the media, the people in power, others around you, who are fearful of letting go of their own conditioning and old programming, awaken yourself to your true potential, and manifest the alternative life which is already here, and waiting for you.

The aim of the matrix, and the system is to drain our energy, this is what the matrix wants. This is why we are exposed to negative news, this is how the matrix feeds itself, and keeps us in line, and where they want us to be.

You need to start making the switch in your mind from negative things, to really positive, nice things, find the positive goals you want to achieve. You need to put your full energy into positive things, and not on the negative things in life. You need to detach from the negative things in life, and raise your spiritual awareness and vibrations.

When you wake in the morning, it is so important that you start every day with positive intentions, don't allow any worries or negativity to come into your mind, and when you leave your houses, don't allow yourself to be affected by other people's negative emotions, rise above that, and detach yourself from emotions, and let negative emotions go.

You have to be fully aware of what is going on around you. Even if people around you are low and negative, don't allow yourself to go down to their vibrations. Raise their vibrations.

The reality transurfer's day has to be a good day, every day. Live in the moment, live in the present. Control your own energy.

Manifest the life you were meant to have, wake up to your potential, and grab the other reality which is already there waiting for you, and manifest the life that you want and deserve.

369 Manifesting & Vision Boards

When you are manifesting what you want in your life you need to practice, practice, practice, and always think positive thoughts which will being positive changes.

If you are not receiving what you ask for, then it is probably because your motivation level is low, your energy is low, and you are not aligning yourself with your goals.

One particular method of manifestation to get the things you want in your life is called the 369 manifestation method.

This method was actually invented by Nikola Tesla. It focuses on 3 numbers, the number three, six and nine, which are also called the divine numbers.

"The key to the universe lies in these three magical numbers, 3,6, and 9. The number 3 directly and potentially links with the universe, whereas the number 6 represents our inner strength, and the number 9, helps let go lf all the negativity and painful past" Nikola Tesla

This method acts as the implementation of the Law of Attraction, which emphasizes focusing on your goals, and dreams with a pattern.

With the 369 method, you need to know what you want to attract whether it be love, a new job, more money etc.

By knowing what you want to attract, you will have an affirmation on what to focus on, which increases the overall success of this method.

The technique is about writing about your goal you want, but like it has already happened to you. i.e., instead of saying "I would like a new car" or "I would like to have a new job which I love" you have to write it as thought you already have it, it has already happened for you, i.e., 'I am so happy I have my new car", or "I am so happy I have my new dream job"

The reason behind this, is that when you see this has already happened, and envision your affirmation coming to fruition, it helps you feel the emotions of that achievement, and compounds the motivation even more.

"To manifest properly, we need to state what we desire in the current situation and tap into the energy of finally achieving it"
Rachel Gibler

The 369 method is all about believing in achieving, and knowing that success is on its way to us.
So what are the 3 steps?
Set your mindset on the affirmation and then do these 3 steps.
1. Write down your affirmation 3x after waking up
2. Write down the affirmation 6x in the afternoon
3. Write down the affirmation 9x before bedtime.

Doing this affirmation all these times is also about repetition, as the human brain is designed to focus more on the things that are repeated on a regular basis. Remember it isn't just about writing the affirmations, but aligning yourself with those goals, and feeling that you already have that in the present tense.

Remember in a previous chapter we discussed there is no past, no future, only the present, and all of the scenarios are already available to us in the present, and that is why we say these affirmations as though we already have what we desire, because we do, just in another reality.

The main benefit of aligning the manifestation process with actions, is the realisation of validity, accuracy and authenticity..

There is no timeline as to when your manifestations will take place, but you need to keep focused, keep affirming what you really want, and keep your energy high, as when your energy dip low the process slows down, and when you start having doubts, then say goodbye to what you want.

It doesn't happen overnight in most cases, and you need to be patient and believe that the universe will provide for you. Your beliefs and intentions have to be strong, and if you do this method as instructed, you will get what you want in your life. The universe will provide for you.

Vision Boards
At this point I just wanted to do a quick overview about another powerful manifestation tool called the vision board.

A vision board is a visual representation of your goals, and the things you want to manifest into your reality. It is a way of getting it out there, so you can see it all the time around you, and you are not just thinking about it, but you are putting it out there.

When you are focusing on the dream job, dream house, dream car, dream life, your brain and subconscious goes into overdrive to bring those things to you.

Using the vision board, and having photos of the things you want, is a fantastic manifesting tool. It needs to be what you actually want.

What you need to write down is everything you want to achieve, and everything you want in your life. You job, your car, your house, holidays, perfect partner, family. what are the most important things you want in your life? What will make your perfect life?

Have at least 10 things on your list that you really want. Then you need to be sure of why you want those things, and be specific why you want these things in your life, and bring into the emotion of why you truly want it.

As for when you want it, there is no timeline with the law of attraction, there is no deadline, but you can have that thought about when you want these things, it doesn't mean that it will happen at that time, but it will happen.

Don't get frustrated, or negative, because then you are sending those thoughts and feelings to the universe, and this affects if you get what you want.

You then need to make this vision board, and make sure that you see this vision board. Put it somewhere prominent, so that you can see it all the time, such as in the kitchen, bedroom, or wherever you will see it all the time.

Your brain responds to everything that you are thinking about, feeling, and its responds the most to your emotions. You need to get the emotions and feelings involved in everything that is on your vision board. Really feel those emotions and feelings. Really imagine what it will be like with those things in your life.

Visualise what your perfect day will be like. Make sure that vision board is always being seen by you, reminding you of the life you are creating.

Don't let other people be negative about what you are doing, as this will send mix messages to the universe. Ignore negativity from other people, and focus and believe in what you want.

The vision board is such a powerful way of manifesting your future and all the things that you want in your life.

Start crating your future right now, and focus on the things that the universe already has in store for you. Remember the things you want on the vision board are already available in a different reality, so manifest them now, and they will come to you.

Here are some quotes about manifestation.

"it's the repetition of affirmations that lead to belief. And once that belief becomes a deep conviction, things begin to happen" Muhammad Ali

"Whether you think you can, or think you can't, you are right" Henry Ford

"Shout to the universe, all good things come to me, and watch your manifestations become your reality" Unknown

"You must assume the feeling of the wish fulfilled until your assumption has all the sensory vividness of reality. You must imagine that you are already experiencing what you desire" Neville Goddard

"Magic is believing in yourself. If you can do that, you can make anything happen" Johann Wolfgang von Goethe

"Your whole life is a manifestation of the thoughts that go on in your head" Lisa Nichols

"You need to see things happening, and envision yourself in a fantasy world, and really believe in that fantasy world, until it comes true" Serena Williams

"Your thoughts have effects that are so great, they create your reality" Dr Joe Dispenza

"You are not your circumstances. You are your possibilities, If you know that, you can do anything"
Oprah Winfrey

"Your life is controlled by what you focus on. That's why you need to focus on where you want to go, not on what you fear" Tony Robbins

"Everything you can imagine is real" Pablo Picasso

"Act as if what you intend to manifest in life is already a reality. Eliminate thoughts of conditions, limitations, or the possibility of it not manifesting. If left undisturbed in your mind, and in the mind of intention simultaneously, it will germinate in the physical world.
Dr Wayne Dyer

"There are no limits to what you can create for you, because your ability to think is unlimited" Rhonda Byrne

"I get everything I want, because I attract it" Ariana Grande

"Our entire biological system, the brain, and the earth itself work on the same frequencies" Nikola Tesla

"Who looks outside, dreams; who looks inside, awakes" Carl Jung

"Create the highest, grandest vision possible for your life, because you become what you believe" Oprah Winfrey

"I must be willing to give up what I am in order to become what I will be" Albert Einstein

"If you don't make peace with your past it will keep showing up in your present. You are what you choose to be today, not what you've chosen before" Dy Wayne Dyer

"We can't solve today's problems with the mentality that created them" Albert Einstein

"We do not need magic to transform our word, we carry all of the power we need inside ourselves already" J.K. Rowling

"The quantum model states that all possibilities exist in this present moment" Dr Joe Dispenza

I have an insane belief in my own ability to manifest things. I believe we are creators, and I believe we create with every thought and word. Every moment is pregnant with the next moment of your life" Jim Carrey

"If you can see it in your head, and you have enough courage to speak it, it will happen. I see the shots, I see the sequences and I don't shy away from them. A lot of times people believe in certain things, but they keep to themselves. They don't put it out there. If you truly believe in it, become vocal with it, you are creating that law of attraction and it will become reality" Conor McGregor

"when you look in the mirror, what do you see? Do you see the real you, or what you have been conditioned to believe is you? The two are so, so different. One is an infinite consciousness capable of being and creating whatever it chooses, the other is an illusion imprisoned by its own perceived and programmed limitations" David Icke

Chapter 28
The Midas system & Millionaire Mindset

"In order to achieve breakthrough results, you need a radical change in your consciousness" Stephen Song

I have done many courses, and workshops in law of attraction and transformation, but the Midas system by Stephen Song is eye opening and enlightening, and I want to share some of those thoughts in this chapter, following on from the law of attraction etc.

If you are earning £1200 per month, a breakthrough is earning £2,000 per month, and remaining at this level. If you are earning £2,000 per month, then a breakthrough is you earning £3,500 per month, and remaining at this level.

You are not able to reach breakthrough results with conventional self-improvement methods.

"In order to achieve breakthrough results, you need radical change in your consciousness"

If you want to earn £100,000 a year, you have got to have a £100,000 a year consciousness. Your life won't get any better unless you take action.

"The principle of connection says that we are not separated human beings, but that we are all connected with each other, and with the universe we live in. We are all one"

The world is an extension of you and your consciousness. Everything in your environment is an extension of you. You can create anything you desire. Everything is a part of you, and this includes abundance, health, and any other material possessions, all these things are already part of you.

Ask, and it is given... at the quantum level, everything you desire is already given to you. All you need to do is to materialize it into your physical world. The subconscious mind needs trust, the more you trust it, the more it will work for you.

See the world as part of you, knowing that whatever you desire is connected to you at quantum level.

"within you is a divine capacity to manifest and attract all that you need or desire" Wayne Dyer

So, are we a body with a soul, or a soul with a body?
We are much more than this physical form that we can see and touch. Within us, there is something eternal. Something that is never born and never dies. This is our soul, or our higher self.
When we see trees our logical mind tells us that there is something within the tree that creates the tree. We find that the tree comes from one small seed. This small seed when opened we find just some brown stuff, which when put under a microscope, we find molecules and atoms. When we put this under the most powerful microscope, we discover there is no particle there, there is just energy, that comes and goes. We are the same, we are just energy, we come from a world of nothingness. We are energy.
The source of creation is dimensionless, it has no boundaries and it is inseparable. We are all one, and the universe is one. The fact is, that we are both a physical body and a non-physical body.
You are not what you observe, you are the observer, this observer is the cause behind everything you observe, it is the origin of everything. You are the creator of your life. You are connected to anything and everything in this universe.

"Manifesting is not about getting things that are not here, it is about attracting what is already here, and is a part of you on a spiritual level" Wayne Dyer

"No matter how persistent the illusion of time is, the illusion of past, present, and future is still an illusion"
Albert Einstein

Now is the only time that exists. By no means can you experience the past or the future, because they don't really exist, they are only a mental concept in the now.

The past and future is only the perception that exists in the human mind. What you think about the past or the future, is just an illusion created by your mind. Now is the only time that really exists. The moments of past, present and future are not separate from each other, they are all happening now. Everything is happening now.

When do you remember your past? You think about it now. When do you dream about your future, you dream it now. You cannot experience the past or the future, because they don't really exist. They are only a mental concept in the Now.

All the so called problems happen in your imaginary future, this is because you experience them and worry about them in your mind, and if you concentrate on what you have to handle in the present moment, you won't experience any problems.

In timeless awareness, you don't experience fear, anxiety or worry because you are in flow, you are one with source energy.

In the magical moment of now, there are an infinite number of things happening, and you can choose to experience any one of them, you make your choice by sending out what you want to the source energy and universe.

The principle of cause and effect says that everything is a cause, that will cause something after it, and everything is an effect that is caused by something before it.

The thing that causes your current circumstances are your inner beliefs and thinking. Your inner world is the cause, and the outer world is the effect. Don't let your outer world fool you. Your inner thoughts and feelings are the causes of your outer conditions. You need to start asking yourself what is the effect of my present thoughts.

Your thoughts cause everything you experience. You have the ability to switch into a positive state with positive thoughts at any time you want to. You are totally responsible for everything that is happening in your life, good or bad.

What you focus on you WILL GET more of. If you focus on more money in your bank you will get it, if you focus on debts and unpaid bills you can be sure that is what you will get more of.

No matter what is happening in your life, you will always be able to find something that you are grateful for and appreciate, and you change your point to positivity at that moment

The real secret, is the way you look at things. If you change the way you look at things, the things you look at will change. Our observation turns that possibility into reality. Everything you see and observe is the cause of everything in your reality. You can change your reality at any time you want to.

If you want something you will always be in that state of wanting it, it will not manifest into your reality. But if you visualise having it, see yourself in the present having it, then it will manifest into your reality.

I know I have said this a number of times in the book, but there is only the now, there is only the present, but there are infinite realities in the now, and everything you want in your life is already there for your in a different reality.

So saying you want something, is looking for the future which doesn't exist. You need to imagine you have it in the only time which is available. The present.

Wanting is a lacking vibration. This leads to the misery of lacking, and having leads to abundance.

To get success in your life, form your own success habits, and the abundance you desire will flow to you. When you are aware of your feelings, you have the ultimate power to change them.

Let's try this exercise. Say this while holding onto a £20 note. "This is a symbol of abundance of the universe that is available to me, I give thanks that 10 times this much is on its way coming back to me now, thank you universe, thank you"

Focus on whatever money you have right now, a £1 or £100,000 both have the same energy, the only different is the size.

Everything is energy, everything around you is energy, money is energy, and if you want money to come to you, you have to make yourself an energy channel that allows that energy to flow to you. You must have an inlet and outlet, you must keep it flowing by giving away the money or spending the money

Tithing is a powerful thing that can attract even more money, and giving your money to people and places that you think need your money the most, certainly helps in attracting more money into your life. Remember you have to have an inlet and outlet.

There is a magic word that can bring you everything you want, and abundance. The word is 'service '. The money that you have is a representation of how much service and value you have provided to others. The better service, and more service you provide, the more wealth you will receive. Develop a rich mindset, and provide a better service to others.

Change your focus from earning more money, to providing a better service, and more service to others.

if you are wanting to be rich, you have to think like the rich. Instead of hating the rich, bless the rich people, because the universe will see that you are liking the rich people, and it will make you rich.

The next time you see someone in your dream house, or driving you dream car, or on dream holiday say these 3 magic words "that's for me", and you are manifesting this from the universe.

The Midas intention technique is a wonderful technique to bring abundance into your life. We have around 60,000 thoughts every day, and most of those thoughts do not support our true purpose and what we want.

The subconscious works on the things that are important to you. What you need to do is write your intentions when you get up in the morning, and before you go to bed every night, and do this every day without fail.

Write the intention like this " I intend to ………..now I accept this or something better" and do this morning and night before bed. After writing your intentions, write "please make this or something better happen in the ways that are for the highest good for me and all concerned. Thank you, thank you"

Do you know what the most important things to do to attract all you desire is?. You need to feel good, happy and blessed, and living a stress free life.

What you need to do is start living your life right now, and getting the things you truly desire right now!

You need to focus…. Live in the now….

There is no other time or moment... just the present... Just now... Start getting everything you want in your life

The Millionaire Mindset
« *Let's imagine for a few moments what our life would be like if we could access, let's say 20% of our brain's capacity, what would that be like?"* Morgan Freeman

Your mindset is quite simply a set of beliefs on how you see the world, and see yourself. What it does do is influence how you think, behave and feel in any given situation. It also impacts on whether you will be successful or a failure. It is the beliefs that a person has about themselves, and their self-perception.

A growth mindset is the belief that you can develop your skills through hard work, and the right strategies, and you are able to change things and expand even further than where you at present.

"Once your mindset changes, everything on the outside will change along with it" Steve Maraboli

Our minds are incredibly powerful and can quite literally create its own reality.

Gratitude

Developing a grateful mindset is where you:-
- Focus on positive life situations
- Turn negative events into positive ones by learning from them and ignoring small everyday negatives.

You can make gratitude a habit by:-
1. Doing nice things for people around you
2. Writing what you are grateful in your life every day
3. Acknowledging the goodness and beauty in your life every day.
4. Find at least one positive thing in every negative situation you encounter.
5. Pick one day of the week where you will NOT complain at all, no matter what happens.
6. Tell you family, friends, children, and people around you that you love them

7. Thank people for the little kind acts they do that you normally take for granted.

8. Eliminate destruction and negative content from your daily life (social media / news)

9. Embrace all of your failures and challenges and see them as a growth lesson

10. Spend more quality time with you friends and family

11. Smile more, laugh more, be happy

STOP chasing happiness, as it is not a destination, it is a by product of all the little things, and small daily actions you do to achieve your goals, on the way to achieving your full potential.

You need to transfer your thoughts into action, keep positive, identify clear actions. A success mindset means being able to take full responsibility for everything that you do, whether it is good or bad.

A daily routine helps you achieve laser like focus from the moment you wake up and get out of bed, to the time you close your eyes and go to sleep.

Before you get out of bed say this sentence...

"Today is going to be a great day"

This over time becomes an habit, and eventually that habit engrains the words in your head every single day.

If you decide to allow someone to get into your head, and for it not to be a great day, then that is on you! Remember it is about perception, and how you perceive events, your thoughts and actions. And you create your own reality. So don't let anyone mess up this sentence, and don't take on board anybody's negativity.

Because, and you know it now, this affects your day, not theirs, and affects what you are giving out to the universe. So keep that in your head, and every single day say "Today is going to be a great day" and do not let anything, or anybody change that.

Everyday visualise the best possible outcomes for things, and saying your goals out loud puts your brain into action.

To get that millionaire mindset, you need to start breaking your day into chunks, because this helps you focus, and be the best. Remember too much time doing one thing, can make you lose interest and focus.

To be able to keep a focused successful mindset, what you eat and drink also helps. Eating the wrong fatty processed foods, soda etc can make you feel sluggish, tired, no energy.

Instead eat foods that have positive effects on your mind and body, including fish, nuts, seeds, avocado, fruit, blueberries, raw carrots and DARK chocolate. Your body and brain will thank you for it.... And replace all of those coffees with drinking water, and cups of tea. Tea has been found to contain polyphenols which are an antioxidant, and anti-inflammatory.

Sleep is massively important with the millionaire mindset, as not getting enough sleep can affect your judgement, ability to retain information and your mood. Also in the long term, sleep deprivation can lead to obesity, diabetes, cardio vascular disease, and even early death.

So to get that good night sleep, limit your coffee fix to earlier in the day, choose foods later in the day that bring on sleep such as bananas, potatoes, oatmeal, darken your room, and don't watch tv or look at your phone for at least an hour before bed.

You must have a burning desire if you want to be successful, and focus. Studies have shown that the best time to program your subconscious mind with ideas is just before going to sleep.

Persistence, will power and desire are key components in becoming successful, and part of the millionaire mindset.

There are 6 steps to a high performance mindset
1. Examine your habits:- are they bringing you closer to the lifestyle you want? Are they serving you in a positive way?
2. Focus on what you can do now:- the most successful people have clarity. Don't waste time and energy thinking about the resources you don't have. Successful people focus on what they want, and how to work within their current environment to achieve those goals.
3. Experiment and experience:- learn new strategies, become adaptable, and experiment.
4. Work with your body:- Play hard, rest hard, plan ahead for healthy meals, self-care and exercise.

5. Traction = taking action:- talk the talk, and walk the walk. Momentum is built through consistent action. Organise your time and follow through on the things that are most important to you

6. Slow down to speed up:- slow down,, because this can actually workout better, as you can take time to come up with step by step plans. Take intentional action to achieve your goals.

There are 4 types of ambitious people. The lost... the frustrated... the procrastinators... and the successful.. the lost, frustrated and procrastinators, all end up in a rut, depressed, unfulfilled, while the successful achieve results others only dream about... which one are you?

There are 3 actions for success

1. Absolute clarity:- be clear on where you are right now, and where you want to be, and have in the future.

2. Intelligent action:- take action that aligned with your values, dreams and goals.

3. Active accountability:- this is about holding your hands up, and being accountable, and responsible for the things that you said you would do, the successes and failures.

Do you know what the 3 best things for amazing relationships, excellent business results and good health are?

1. Getting the best sleep:- your bedroom has to become your sanctuary. It should be peaceful and relaxing. De-clutter your room, get the TV and computers out of there, make sure your room is dark, eliminate all noises, and room at optional temperature.

2. Drink more water, no hearty meals at night or certainly not less than 4 hours before bed, no caffeine after 3pm, no TV or screen time for at least an hour before bed, preferably no alcohol,

3. Have an evening routine for the next day that includes (a) review of the day (b) clothes for the next day (c) bathroom necessities (d) meditation, self-relaxation, positive affirmations.

Morning routine
1. Gratitude for extraordinary day ahead.
2. Drink hot water with lemon and turmeric as this improves your digestion, helps release liver bile, strengthens immune system, adjusts body's pH level, and more energy.
3. Meditation or breathwork.
4. Miracle shower:- alternating warm and cold throughout the shower. This warm water helps with muscle relaxation, reduces blood pressure, and decreases anxiety.. the cold water stimulates the immune system, increases attention levels, stimulates metabolism, clears the mind,
5. Have Breakfast:- the best breakfast is a smoothie, because it is nutritious and fast.
6. Journalling:- this is about staying connected to yourself
7. Only one:- this is about picking one piece of the most important project of that particular day.
8. 12 month goals:- every morning write list of 12 goals.
9. Relationship note:- Write a note for your partner which will brighten up your partners day. Write a compliment, or something else which will make them happy for the day.

The optimal times to go to bed are really between 9-10 pm and wake up 4am or 5am. There are many reasons to wake up at 5am, and here are just a few.
1. You become a 1% er, and you have the opportunity to spend quality time with yourself.
2. Nobody bothers you at 5am with calls, emails.
3. You can get out into nature for a walk or run.
4. You can create a strategic plan for your business
5. You can watch the sunrise.
6. You can watch inspirational videos or read a book.
7. You can prepare yourself and get ready and have more time for yourself in the morning.
8. You can meditate or do some breathwork
9. You can set your intentions regarding the new day ahead.

10. You can make breakfast for partner and kids

11. You can repeat affirmations, and focus on your vision board

12. You start your day with proactive energy rather than reactive

13. You have enough time to practice Ho'oponopono

14. You can write your goals for the next 12 months on a daily basis

15. You can write for 15 minutes about all the things you are grateful for.

The millionaire mindset chapter, is just an extension of the other chapters in part 3. It is an important part of getting the right positive mindset, changing your current beliefs and coding, and focusing on getting the best possible life you want, and manifesting everything that you want in your life. Remember the only thing that is holding you back from the life you want is your thoughts, emotions and perceptions. It is never too late to realise your goals, get your dream job, house, car, and become the person you always wanted to be.

Conclusion

I hope you enjoyed this book, as much as I enjoyed writing it, and it motivates you to go and look deeper into what we are made of, and how you can change your lives, and heal yourself from any dis-ease, and have a better understanding how this can happen through the wonderful fields of Neuroplasticity and Epigenetics.

It is my passion to help people get the best out of their lives, and heal themselves naturally, and not become lifetime patients of Western Medicine, and long term clients of the Pharmaceutical companies making billions from dis-ease.

This is not taking away anything from the wonderful doctors, nurses, Health Care Assistants, and other professionals working in hospitals all around the world, as most of them are wonderful caring people, who give their lives to caring for their patients and supporting them to get better.

This book is about taking back your own lives, realising that it is YOU, who holds the key to better health.

It is YOU who holds they key to healing YOURSELF from dis-ease, mental health, and stress, and it is YOU who can change your life around TODAY.

By realising who, and what you are, and how powerful your mind is, and also realising that we are all connected, and we all have the key to the Universe and whatever we want in this life. It is already there for waiting for you.

If you need help with any issues, trauma, stress, mental health. If you are a business wanting to help your employees with stress and mental health. If you would like to attend the 3 day workshop or any of the other workshops in future, please contact us in the following ways.

Website:- www.thevikingbuddha.com
Email:- thevikingbuddha@yahoo.com

Or telephone :- 0330 043 3203

Finally, I wish every single person good health, and hope that you find your purpose in this life, and manifest each and every goal, and dream to make your life, the life YOU deserve.

Namaste, Aloha, and Love and Light to you all

www.ingramcontent.com/pod-product-compliance
Lightning Source LLC
Chambersburg PA
CBHW070352120526
44590CB00014B/1098